Contents

Introduction to the Student   4

How to Use This Book   6

Instructions for the Pacing Drills   8

Steps to Faster Reading

    Step 1: Preview   9

    Step 2: Read for Meaning   10

    Step 3: Grasp Paragraph Sense   11

    Step 4: Organize Facts   12

Timed Reading Selections   15

Answer Key   116

Progress Graph   118

Pacing Graph   120

Introduction to the Student

These *Timed Readings* are designed to help you become a faster and better reader. As you progress through the book, you will find yourself growing in reading speed and comprehension. You will be challenged to increase your reading rate while maintaining a high level of comprehension.

Reading, like most things, improves with practice. If you practice improving your reading speed, you will improve. As you will see, the rewards of improved reading speed will be well worth your time and effort.

Why Read Faster?

The quick and simple answer is that faster readers are better readers. Does this statement surprise you? You might think that fast readers would miss something and their comprehension might suffer. This is not true, for two reasons:

1. Faster readers comprehend faster. When you read faster, the writer's message is coming to you faster and makes sense sooner. Ideas are interconnected. The writer's thoughts are all tied together, each one leading to the next. The more quickly you can see how ideas are related to each other, the more quickly you can comprehend the meaning of what you are reading.

2. Faster readers concentrate better. Concentration is essential for comprehension. If your mind is wandering you can't understand what you are reading. A lack of concentration causes you to re-read, sometimes over and over, in order to comprehend. Faster readers concentrate better because there's less time for distractions to interfere. Comprehension, in turn, contributes to concentration. If you are concentrating and comprehending, you will not become distracted.

Want to Read More?

Do you wish that you could read more? (or, at least, would you like to do your required reading in less time?) Faster reading will help.

The illustration on the next page shows the number of books someone might read over a period of ten years. Let's see what faster reading could do for you. Look at the stack of books read by a slow reader and the stack

4

TIMED READINGS

Third Edition

Fifty 400-Word Passages
with Questions for
Building Reading Speed

BOOK THREE

Edward Spargo

Jamestown Publishers

Providence, Rhode Island

Titles in This Series
Timed Readings, Third Edition
Timed Readings in Literature

Teaching Notes are available for this text and
will be sent to the instructor. Please write on
school stationery; tell us what grade
you teach and identify the text.

Timed Readings, Third Edition
Book Three

Catalog No. 903

© 1989 by Jamestown Publishers, Inc.

Cover and text design by Deborah Hulsey Christie

Printed in the United States of America

6 7 8 HS 97 96 95 94

ISBN 0-89061-505-5

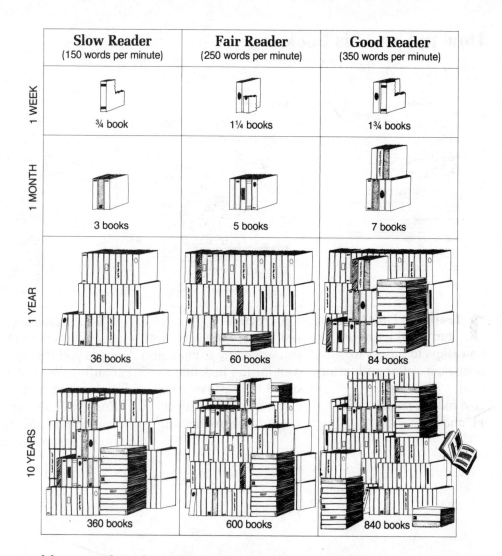

	Slow Reader (150 words per minute)	Fair Reader (250 words per minute)	Good Reader (350 words per minute)
1 WEEK	¾ book	1¼ books	1¾ books
1 MONTH	3 books	5 books	7 books
1 YEAR	36 books	60 books	84 books
10 YEARS	360 books	600 books	840 books

read by a good reader. (We show a speed of 350 words a minute for our "good" reader, but many fast readers can more than double that speed.) Let's say, however, that you are now reading at a rate of 150 words a minute. The illustration shows you reading 36 books a year. By increasing your reading speed to 250 words a minute, you could increase the number of books to 60 a year.

We have arrived at these numbers by assuming that the readers in our illustration read for one hour a day, six days a week, and that an average book is about 72,000 words long. Many people do not read that much, but they might if they could learn to read better and faster.

Faster reading doesn't *take* time, it *saves* time!

How to Use This Book

1 Learn the Four Steps
Study and learn the four steps to follow to become a better and faster reader. The steps are covered on pages 9, 10, 11, and 12.

2 Preview
Turn to the selection you are going to read and wait for the instructor's signal to preview. Your instructor will allow 30 seconds for previewing.

3 Begin reading
When your instructor gives you the signal, begin reading. Read at a slightly faster-than-normal speed. Read well enough so that you will be able to answer questions about what you have read.

7 Fill in the progress graph
Enter your score and plot your reading time on the graph on page 118 or 119. The right-hand side of the graph shows your words-per-minute reading speed. Write this number at the bottom of the page on the line labeled *Words per Minute*.

4 Record your time
When you finish reading, look at the blackboard and note your reading time. Your reading time will be the lowest time remaining on the board, or the next number to be erased. Write this time at the bottom of the page on the line labeled *Reading Time*.

5 Answer the questions
Answer the ten questions on the next page. There are five fact questions and five thought questions. Pick the *best* answer to each question and put an x in the box beside it.

6 Correct your answers
Using the Answer Key on pages 116 and 117, correct your work. Circle your wrong answers and put an x in the box you should have marked. Score 10 points for each correct answer. Write your score at the bottom of the page on the line labeled *Comprehension Score*.

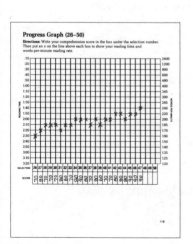

Instructions for the Pacing Drills

From time to time your instructor may wish to conduct pacing drills using *Timed Readings*. For this work you need to use the Pacing Dots printed in the margins of your book pages. The dots will help you regulate your reading speed to match the pace set by your instructor or announced on the reading cassette tape.

Pacing Dots

You will be reading at the correct pace if you are at the dot when your instructor says "Mark" or when you hear a tone on the tape. If you are ahead of the pace, read a little more slowly; if you are behind the pace, increase your reading speed. Try to match the pace exactly.

Follow these steps.

Step 1: Record the pace. At the bottom of the page, write on the line labeled *Words per Minute* the rate announced by the instructor or by the speaker on the tape.

Step 2: Begin reading. Wait for the signal to begin reading. Read at a slightly faster-than-normal speed. You will not know how on-target your pace is until you hear your instructor say "Mark" or until you hear the first tone on the tape. After a little practice you will be able to select an appropriate starting speed most of the time.

Step 3: Adjust your pace. As you read, try to match the pace set by the instructor or the tape. Read more slowly or more quickly as necessary. You should be reading the line beside the dot when you hear the pacing signal. The pacing sounds may distract you at first. Don't worry about it. Keep reading and your concentration will return.

Step 4: Stop and answer questions. Stop reading when you are told to, even if you have not finished the selection. Answer the questions right away. Correct your work and record your score on the line *Comprehension Score*. Strive to maintain 80 percent comprehension on each drill as you gradually increase your pace.

Step 5: Fill in the pacing graph. Transfer your words-per-minute rate to the box labeled *Pace* on the pacing graph on page 120. Then plot your comprehension score on the line above the box.

These pacing drills are designed to help you become a more flexible reader. They encourage you to "break out" of a pattern of reading everything at the same speed.

The drills help in other ways, too. Sometimes in a reading program you reach a certain level and bog down. You don't seem able to move on and progress. The pacing drills will help you to work your way out of such slumps and get your reading program moving again.

Steps to Faster Reading

STEP 1: PREVIEW

When you read, do you start in with the first word, or do you look over the whole selection for a moment? Good readers preview the selection first—this helps to make them good, and fast, readers.

1. Read the Title. The first thing to do when previewing is to read the title of the selection. Titles are designed not only to announce the subject, but also to make the reader think. What can you learn from the title? What thoughts does it bring to mind? What do you already know about this subject?

2. Read the Opening Paragraph. If the first paragraph is long, read the first sentence or two instead. The first paragraph is the writer's opportunity to greet the reader. He may have something to tell you about what is to come. Some writers announce what they hope to tell you in the selection. Some writers tell why they are writing. Some writers just try to get the reader's attention—they may ask a provocative question.

3. Read the Closing Paragraph. If the last paragraph is long, read just the final line or two. The closing paragraph is the writer's last chance to talk to his reader. He may have something important to say at the end. Some writers repeat the main idea once more. Some writers draw a conclusion: this is what they have been leading up to. Some writers summarize their thoughts; they tie all the facts together.

4. Glance Through. Scan the selection quickly to see what else you can pick up. Discover whatever you can to help you read the selection. Are there names, dates, numbers? If so, you may have to read more slowly. Are there colorful adjectives? The selection might be light and fairly easy to read. Is the selection informative, containing a lot of facts, or conversational, an informal discussion with the reader?

flying
normal
towers
stage
migration.
some
cruising
pelicans,
time
subtle
scientists
close

Steps to Faster Reading

STEP 2: READ FOR MEANING

When you read, do you just see words? Are you so occupied reading words that you sometimes fail to get the meaning? Good readers see beyond the words—they read for meaning. This makes them faster readers.

1. Build Concentration. You cannot read with understanding if you are not concentrating. Every reader's mind wanders occasionally; it is not a cause for alarm. When you discover that your thoughts have strayed, correct the situation right away. The longer you wait, the harder it becomes. Avoid distractions and distracting situations. Outside noises and activities will compete for your attention if you let them. Keep the preview information in mind as you read. This will help to focus your attention on the selection.

2. Read in Thought Groups. Individual words do not tell us much. They must be combined with other words in order to yield meaning. To obtain meaning from the printed page, therefore, the reader should see the words in meaningful combinations. If you see only a word at a time (called word-by-word reading), your comprehension suffers along with your speed. To improve both speed and comprehension, try to group the words into phrases which have a natural relationship to each other. For practice, you might want to read aloud, trying to speak the words in meaningful combinations.

3. Question the Author. To sustain the pace you have set for yourself, and to maintain a high level of comprehension, question the writer as you read. Continually ask yourself such questions as, "What does this mean? What is he saying now? How can I use this information?" Questions like these help you to concentrate fully on the selection.

Steps to Faster Reading

STEP 3: GRASP
PARAGRAPH SENSE

The paragraph is the basic unit of meaning. If you can discover quickly and understand the main point of each paragraph, you can comprehend the author's message. Good readers know how to find the main ideas of paragraphs quickly. This helps to make them faster readers.

1. Find the Topic Sentence. The topic sentence, the sentence containing the main idea, is often the first sentence of a paragraph. It is followed by other sentences which support, develop, or explain the main idea. Sometimes a topic sentence comes at the end of a paragraph. When it does, the supporting details come first, building the base for the topic sentence. Some paragraphs do not have a topic sentence. Such paragraphs usually create a mood or feeling, rather than present information.

2. Understand Paragraph Structure. Every well-written paragraph has purpose. The purpose may be to inform, define, explain, persuade, compare or contrast, illustrate, and so on. The purpose should always relate to the main idea and expand on it. As you read each paragraph, see how the body of the paragraph is used to tell you more about the main idea or topic sentence. Read the supporting details intelligently, recognizing that what you are reading is all designed to develop the single main idea.

Steps to Faster Reading

STEP 4: ORGANIZE FACTS

When you read, do you tend to see a lot of facts without any apparent connection or relationship? Understanding how the facts all fit together to deliver the author's message is, after all, the reason for reading. Good readers organize facts as they read. This helps them to read rapidly and well.

1. Discover the Writer's Plan. Look for a clue or signal word early in the article which might reveal the author's structure. Every writer has a plan or outline which he follows. If the reader can discover his method of organization, he has the key to understanding the message. Sometimes the author gives you obvious signals. If he says, "There are three reasons . . ." the wise reader looks for a listing of the three items. Other less obvious signal words such as *moreover, otherwise, consequently* all tell the reader the direction the writer's message will take.

2. Relate as You Read. As you read the selection, keep the information learned during the preview in mind. See how the ideas you are reading all fit into place. Consciously strive to relate what you are reading to the title. See how the author is carrying through in his attempt to piece together a meaningful message. As you discover the relationship among the ideas, the message comes through quickly and clearly.

**Timed
Reading
Selections**

1 Keep It Soaring

No one knows for sure just how old kites are. We do know that they were in use centuries ago. But we do not know for certain when kites were first flown. Greek stories tell of kites four centuries before Christ. In Korea, legend links the kite to warfare. It is said that a general used a kite to excite his army. A lantern attached to the kite looked like a new star to the troops. This star was thought to be a sign of good luck from the heavens.

Twenty-five centuries ago, kites were well known in China. These first kites were probably made of wood. They may even have been covered with silk because silk was in use at that time. About five centuries later, the Chinese learned how to make paper from vegetable fibers. This may have been used as a cover for early kites, too.

Early kites were built for certain uses. In ancient China, they were used to carry ropes across rivers and canyons. Once across, the ropes were tied down and wooden bridges were hung from them. Legend tells of one general who flew musical kites over the enemy camp. The enemy fled, believing the sounds to be the warning voices of angels. Legend tells of manned kites, too. These were used to drop men behind enemy lines. Manned kites were used to carry soldiers to spy on the enemy.

Kite flying later became a national pastime in China. In the first and second centuries, kites of different shapes came into being. Kites were also made to look like men, birds, animals, and monsters. Some designs were very beautiful.

Many people flew kites in Europe by the fifteenth century. Marco Polo may have brought the kite back from his visit to China.

The kite has been linked to great names and events. For instance, Ben Franklin used a kite to prove that lightning is electricity. He flew the kite in a storm. He did this in order to draw the lightning from the clouds. He tied a metal key and a strip of silk to the kite line. The silk ribbon would stop the lightning from passing through his body. Ben's idea was first laughed at. But later on, it led to the invention of the lightning rod.

With such grand history, kite flying is sure to continue to remain an entertaining and popular sport.

Recalling Facts

1. How many centuries before
   Christ did Greek stories tell
   of kites?
   ☐ a. two
   ☐ b. three
   ☐ c. four

2. In what country were kites
   linked to warfare?
   ☐ a. America
   ☐ b. Greece
   ☐ c. Korea

3. The first Chinese kites were
   probably made of
   ☐ a. cotton.
   ☐ b. leaves.
   ☐ c. wood.

4. The Chinese learned how to
   make paper from
   ☐ a. melted sand.
   ☐ b. pine sap.
   ☐ c. vegetable fiber.

5. Marco Polo may have brought
   the kite to Europe from
   ☐ a. China.
   ☐ b. India.
   ☐ c. Korea.

Understanding the Passage

6. What is this article
   mostly about?
   ☐ a. The history of kites
   ☐ b. How kites are made
   ☐ c. Famous kite builders

7. We can see that kites
   were invented
   ☐ a. long before the birth
        of Christ.
   ☐ b. just after the birth
        of Christ.
   ☐ c. many years after the
        birth of Christ.

8. This article hints that silk was
   invented before
   ☐ a. ink.
   ☐ b. iron.
   ☐ c. paper.

9. Kites were once used
   to help build
   ☐ a. boats.
   ☐ b. bridges.
   ☐ c. churches.

10. One general used musical kites
    in order to
    ☐ a. amuse the enemy.
    ☐ b. help the enemy.
    ☐ c. frighten the enemy.

2   A Body Without a Head

Soon after the Declaration of Independence was signed, the Continental Congress drew up a plan for a central government. The plan was called *The Articles of Confederation and Perpetual Union*. It was sent to the states. They were asked to accept it.

Many of the states did not like the plan. Some said that the central government would not be strong enough. Other states feared that they would lose the right to govern their own people. Changes were made in the plan. It was accepted by all of the thirteen states by March 1, 1781.

Under the Articles of Confederation, the states entered into "a firm league of friendship" with one another. The people in each state thought of the other states as friends. They would help one another. But the people did not think that they were members of a true Union.

The Articles of Confederation set up a Congress of one House only. Each state was represented in that House. Each state had only one vote.

The Congress had power to make war and peace. It could make money. A committee of the Congress governed the nation when the Congress was not meeting.

After the war was won, the purpose in working together was gone. The war had held the states together to win freedom. Many of the people thought that the Union had ended. The states fought with one another.

The central government did not have enough power to carry on its work. The Congress could do nothing unless the states agreed. For example, the Congress asked the states for money, but could not force them to pay. The Congress could not tax the citizens. The Congress asked the states to send soldiers to protect the nation. But some of the states refused. The Congress made treaties with other countries. But the states did not obey the treaties.

The Articles of Confederation was weak in other ways. There was no President. The central government was "a body without a head." There were no federal courts. The Congress could not force any person to obey the laws.

The Congress had no power to control trade among the states or between the states and foreign countries. The states fought over the right to tax goods from other states. Also, the states fought over the ownership of certain lands. Virginia and Maryland could not agree about which state owned Chesapeake Bay.

Recalling Facts

1. How many states accepted the Articles of Confederation?
   - ☐ a. nine
   - ☐ b. thirteen
   - ☐ c. fifteen

2. The Articles of Confederation was accepted in the year
   - ☐ a. 1776.
   - ☐ b. 1781.
   - ☐ c. 1812.

3. In Congress, each state was given
   - ☐ a. one vote.
   - ☐ b. two votes.
   - ☐ c. three votes.

4. The author mentions the state of
   - ☐ a. Florida.
   - ☐ b. Maine.
   - ☐ c. Virginia.

5. The Articles of Confederation was drawn up by the
   - ☐ a. President.
   - ☐ b. Continental Congress.
   - ☐ c. New England states.

Understanding the Passage

6. Under the Articles of Confederation, the government could set up a
   - ☐ a. postal department.
   - ☐ b. welfare department.
   - ☐ c. treasury department.

7. Just after the Articles of Confederation was accepted,
   - ☐ a. the United States waged war on England.
   - ☐ b. a President was elected.
   - ☐ c. the states began to argue among themselves.

8. One drawback to the Articles of Confederation was that it did not
   - ☐ a. create courts.
   - ☐ b. allow Congress to declare war.
   - ☐ c. allow Congress to ask states for money.

9. The phrase "body without a head" means a
   - ☐ a. state without a capital.
   - ☐ b. senator without power.
   - ☐ c. government without a President.

10. The Articles of Confederation was written
    - ☐ a. before the Declaration of Independence was signed.
    - ☐ b. during the Revolutionary War.
    - ☐ c. after the Declaration of Independence was signed.

Supplying energy to support the many workings of the body is one of the chief jobs of food. This energy comes from the fats, carbohydrates, and proteins in foods. Of the three, fat is the most concentrated source. It gives more than twice as much energy for its weight as protein or carbohydrates do.

Alcohol also supplies energy and is second to fat as a source. It provides about three-fourths as much energy as an equal weight of fat.

Food energy is counted in calories. All foods furnish calories. Some furnish much less in one serving than others. Foods that contain large amounts of water are quite low in calories. Water, which has no calories, dilutes the nutrients in these foods. Many fresh fruits and vegetables are in this category. Calories climb, however, when sugar, fat, or a fat-containing food such as salad dressing or cream is added.

Foods rich in fat, starch, or sugar, and drinks high in alcohol are high in calories.

When one chooses foods that have more calories than needed, the extra energy is stored in the body as fat. Overeating all the time can lead to a gain in weight. If too little food is eaten to meet energy needs, the body's stored fat serves as an energy source. Weight loss results when there is a shortage of food day after day.

Weight stays about the same when the energy from food matches the energy needs of the body.

It is best to keep one's weight right for one's height, at all ages, even during childhood. There are two rules that one can use.

Food intake should be reduced as one becomes less active. Exercise and activity burn up calories. If a person cuts down on activity but doesn't cut down on food, he is getting more energy than the body needs. The extra calories are stored by the body in the form of fat.

Food intake should be reduced without shortchanging the body of nutrients. Crash diets and food fads are not the answer and may be dangerous to health. A person should cut down on food but should not cut out any important kinds of foods.

Snacks are counted as a part of the day's total food. Some snacks can help meet nutritional needs, but eating between meals often leads to more calories than are needed.

Recalling Facts

1. The most concentrated source
   of energy is
   ☐ a. proteins.
   ☐ b. carbohydrates.
   ☐ c. fats.

2. Foods that are low in calories
   contain large amounts of
   ☐ a. water.
   ☐ b. alcohol.
   ☐ c. starch.

3. If you cut down on activity but
   not on food, you will
   ☐ a. gain weight.
   ☐ b. lose weight.
   ☐ c. stay the same.

4. Energy is stored by the body
   in the form of
   ☐ a. muscle.
   ☐ b. fat.
   ☐ c. blood cells.

5. The author mentions that
   weight should be watched
   even in
   ☐ a. old age.
   ☐ b. childhood.
   ☐ c. adolescence.

Understanding the Passage

6. The calorie count is highest in
   ☐ a. oranges.
   ☐ b. butter.
   ☐ c. beer.

7. According to the author, a
   person on a diet
   ☐ a. could drink wine with meals.
   ☐ b. should cut down on
      protein intake.
   ☐ c. could snack between meals.

8. The author implies that an adult
   ☐ a. needs the same number of
      calories as an adolescent.
   ☐ b. should decrease his con-
      sumption of cereal grains.
   ☐ c. requires fewer calories as he
      grows older.

9. A diet devised by the author
   would be based on
   ☐ a. water, fats, and cereals.
   ☐ b. fresh fruits, butter, and eggs.
   ☐ c. proteins, fats, and
      carbohydrates.

10. We can conclude that
    ☐ a. most doctors discourage
       dieting.
    ☐ b. crash diets are popular
       among young people.
    ☐ c. the most effective diets are
       carefully planned.

The Pathfinder

When we found him, he was a sorry sight. His clothes were torn, his hands bleeding. Before we reached him, we saw him fall. He lay a moment. Then he pulled himself to his feet, staggered a few yards through the woods and fell again. When we lifted him off the ground, he tried to break away and run, like a wild animal.

After we got him out, we went back to find the gun that he had thrown down. His tracks showed that for two days he had circled in the forest, within 200 yards of the road. His senses were so dulled by fear and exhaustion that he did not hear the cars going by or see the lights at night.

We found him just in time.

This man, like others before him, had simply panicked when he knew he was lost. What had been a near disaster might have turned out as only a pleasant walk, had he taken a few precautions before he stepped from the highway or off a known trail.

Whatever sense of direction that a man may claim, it's still largely a question of observation. Both consciously and subconsciously, a woodsman keeps an eye on his surroundings. He notes the shape of a mountain, the direction water flows through a swamp, and many little traits about every trail he travels—how a tree leans across it, an uprooted stump, a rockslide. He sees the way the ridges run, the flow of the streams. With these in mind, he may be turned around many times, but he is seldom lost.

There are exceptions, of course, and once in a while a man does get involved in some strange problem that puts him into the "lost" column. A rainstorm or sudden blizzard may catch him without a compass in his pocket. Darkness may find him in a rugged area, where travel is dangerous without a light.

When this happens, the normal first reaction is the dread of embarrassment as a result of his poor woodsmanship. He may also be concerned about the inconvenience that he will cause his friends when he doesn't show up. This false pride may lead him to keep on the move in a false effort to find his way against all odds.

The person who thinks ahead is seldom in great danger. He'll be safe if he observes carefully, thinks ahead, and remains calm.

---

*Reading Time*_____ *Comprehension Score*_____ *Words per Minute*_____

Recalling Facts

1. How many days had the lost man circled in the forest?
   - ☐ a. two
   - ☐ b. four
   - ☐ c. six

2. How close had the man been to a road during the time he was lost?
   - ☐ a. 100 yards
   - ☐ b. 200 yards
   - ☐ c. 300 yards

3. The man did not know that cars were passing by because he was
   - ☐ a. exhausted.
   - ☐ b. blind.
   - ☐ c. deaf.

4. Finding your way in the woods is largely a question of
   - ☐ a. intelligence.
   - ☐ b. observation.
   - ☐ c. endurance.

5. The man is described as a "sorry sight" because of his
   - ☐ a. prayerful kneeling.
   - ☐ b. loud crying.
   - ☐ c. bleeding hands.

Understanding the Passage

6. The author suggests that if the man had not been found, he would have
   - ☐ a. become completely disoriented.
   - ☐ b. run onto the highway.
   - ☐ c. been attacked by wild animals.

7. The first thing that the author saw when he found the man was
   - ☐ a. the man's torn clothes.
   - ☐ b. the remains of a campfire.
   - ☐ c. a crude signal for help.

8. After they found the man, they went back to find the man's
   - ☐ a. family.
   - ☐ b. canoe.
   - ☐ c. weapon.

9. The author tells the story of the lost man as an example of
   - ☐ a. people who panic when they think they are lost.
   - ☐ b. hunters who go into the woods alone.
   - ☐ c. people who do not know how to signal for help properly.

10. According to the article, a good woodsman
    - ☐ a. takes notice of details along the trail.
    - ☐ b. knows the type of clouds passing overhead.
    - ☐ c. tells other people where he is going.

5   Color Them New

What sells cars every year is newness. And what defines "newness" today is color. The cars themselves are "new" each year. But most of what's new is hidden.

One of the most important signals—the thing that tells the consumer at first glance that this is a new car—is color. Forty years ago, newness was signaled by a set of fins in the showroom. Cars weren't exactly colorful, but they didn't have to be. What the paints lacked in style, the designers made up for with sheet metal and chrome.

That situation has almost been reversed today. It's a reversal that began in the mid-'50s with the use of the "two-tones," especially with the first good "whites" as the second tone.

This change was caused by a lot of things. One of the most important can be summed up in one word: costs. Costs have helped rule out major body style changes every two years. And the internal changes have added still other costs.

But this glamour isn't something that happened just because somebody's costs went up. It happened because our methods improved. We can make much better finishes now than we could thirty years ago. They're more exciting to see. They last longer. And they're easier to work with on the production line. The result is that we can come up with new colors that will help sell cars.

There isn't any mystery in what colors will sell. There's a lot of talk about the psychology of color. But it does not really apply in the car-color business. The important thing is to use a color that the public hasn't seen before, or that has been forgotten.

In the early 1950s, light blue was the most popular. Light and medium greens ran close behind. And one of every ten cars was black.

Ten years later, white had taken over. And from 1959 to 1963, nearly 20 percent of cars were white. Since then, color schemes have included earth tones, bright metallic colors, and repeats of old hues.

New colors for cars are the product of a complex effort by automobile stylists, researchers developing new pigments, researchers and stylists in the finishes industry, and the people on the production lines.

So the new vibrant car colors we see result from a complex process organized to develop new finishes, finishes that are not only different but tasteful and workable.

Recalling Facts

1. In the sale of cars today, "newness" means
   □ a. styling.
   □ b. performance.
   □ c. color.

2. What factor has ruled out major body style changes every two years?
   □ a. production problems
   □ b. public taste
   □ c. cost

3. "Two-tones" were first introduced in the middle
   □ a. 1940s.
   □ b. 1950s.
   □ c. 1960s.

4. During the early 1950s the most popular car color was
   □ a. blue.
   □ b. white.
   □ c. black.

5. The most popular colors today are
   □ a. vibrant.
   □ b. bright metallics.
   □ c. multi-tones.

Understanding the Passage

6. Forty years ago, "newness" was indicated by
   □ a. design.
   □ b. horsepower.
   □ c. color.

7. Glamorous cars are mostly the result of
   □ a. the demands of the buying public.
   □ b. the preferences of industry executives.
   □ c. advancements and discoveries in science.

8. Finishes on cars today
   □ a. are more difficult to work with on the assembly line.
   □ b. last longer than they did 30 years ago.
   □ c. require more care than they once did.

9. The "psychology of color"
   □ a. plays an important role in the auto industry.
   □ b. has no bearing on the purchase of cars.
   □ c. is not mentioned in the article.

10. This article does not mention
    □ a. the history of car colors.
    □ b. who is responsible for new colors.
    □ c. color preferences in used cars.

A Cord of Wood

Where can I get good firewood? How is it sold? What safety measures should be taken when burning firewood? Is the fireplace good for home heating?

These are just a few of the questions that need answering for the many people who plan to make greater use of the home fireplace.

A fireplace gives off radiant heat that can bring quick comfort to a cold or damp room. In spring and fall, a fire will drive away early morning and evening chills less expensively than a large heating system. Less fuel is used and a large amount of heat is quickly produced. Should storms or power failures interrupt the normal means of heating and cooking, a fireplace is something that is very handy to have.

A fireplace, however, is not the best means of producing heat for the home. An open fireplace draws large amounts of warm air from the home; this warm air is then replaced by cold outside air. Modern wood-burning stoves that have automatic draft controls are more efficient. They draw smaller amounts of air. These stoves are often sold in rural areas.

Some fuels are pollution and health hazards, but wood is much lower in irritating pollutants than most fuels. Most people generally link wood smoke with the past. Wood smoke in the air makes our visits to old villages seem all the more pleasant.

Wood has a low ash content. It burns cleanly, leaving only a minimum of waste as ash. The ash that remains can be mixed with the soil and can be a valuable fertilizer.

Wood is a renewable fuel resource. Coal, oil, and gas are limited re-sources; once used, they cannot be replaced. But new trees can be grown. And after a few years, more wood is ready to use. Wood can be found in many places, can be easily cut, and is quite inexpensive.

The wood that you use in your fireplace might very well be unusable in any other way. By burning it in your fireplace, you can help reduce the piles of wood waste in woodlands, city dumps, and around wood indus-tries. Using it for firewood puts it to good use.

Generally, a standard cord of air dry, dense hardwood weighs about two tons. It provides as much heat as one ton of coal, 175 gallons of No. 2 fuel oil, or 24,000 cubic feet of natural gas.

Recalling Facts

1. A fireplace draws from the home
   - ☐ a. cold air.
   - ☐ b. moist air.
   - ☐ c. warm air.

2. Wood ash can be used to
   - ☐ a. melt ice.
   - ☐ b. fertilize gardens.
   - ☐ c. remove grease stains.

3. Compared with other fuels, wood
   - ☐ a. burns cleanly.
   - ☐ b. is expensive.
   - ☐ c. burns slowly.

4. A cord of hardwood usually weighs about
   - ☐ a. one ton.
   - ☐ b. two tons.
   - ☐ c. three tons.

5. A cord of wood provides as much heat as
   - ☐ a. 50 gallons of oil.
   - ☐ b. 100 gallons of oil.
   - ☐ c. 175 gallons of oil.

Understanding the Passage

6. When the author says that wood is a renewable fuel resource, he means that
   - ☐ a. trees grow back where others have been cut down.
   - ☐ b. it does not have to be bought from foreign countries.
   - ☐ c. it does not have to be dug out of the ground like coal.

7. This article is mostly about burning wood in
   - ☐ a. specially built stoves.
   - ☐ b. fireplaces.
   - ☐ c. furnaces.

8. According to the author, a fireplace heats a room
   - ☐ a. quickly.
   - ☐ b. gradually.
   - ☐ c. evenly.

9. Wood-burning stoves
   - ☐ a. do not create as much draft in rooms as fireplaces do.
   - ☐ b. are more expensive to install than fireplaces are.
   - ☐ c. use less wood than fireplaces do.

10. We can conclude that
    - ☐ a. breathing wood smoke can cause serious illness.
    - ☐ b. fireplaces should be used to heat homes.
    - ☐ c. wood should be used more commonly as a source of heat.

7   A Sticky Wicket

Three very different games top the British sports scene—association football, rugby football, and cricket.

Association football is similar to our soccer.

Rugby football is known as the great-grandfather of American-style football, but rougher. There is plenty of tackling, running, passing, and kicking. Hardly any protective gear is worn. The forward pass is not allowed, but passing backward is allowed. The action takes on the appearance of a basketball game at times. The ball is a little rounder than our football.

Cricket is to the British what baseball is to Americans. In both games players use a ball and bat and score runs.

In cricket, two wickets are set up 22 yards apart on the playing field. A wicket consists of three thin poles on which two peg-shaped objects called "bails" are placed. The team at bat sends a man to stand in front of each wicket. Each in turn "defends" his wicket from being knocked over by the bowler's ball.

There are two bowlers. One bowls six times against the wicket at one end of the field, then fields while the pitcher at the opposite end bowls.

The batter hits each pitched ball to keep it from knocking over his wicket. However, he has a choice of running or not running. If he hits a long ball and runs, his batting partner at the opposite end of the field also runs. The batters run carrying their bats. They must touch the bats to a "crease" marked off in front of each wicket. Then they must return to their own wicket before the ball has been fielded and thrown back in an attempt to knock a wicket down.

If the batters are successful, two runs are scored.

A batter is "out" if he hits a fly that is caught, if he is touched by a pitched ball, if he fails to complete his run, or if his wicket is knocked down. When ten of a team's eleven players have been "out," the opposing team comes to bat.

Because the batter has the choice of running or not running, he may remain at bat for hours. Good batters do just that to wear out the bowlers.

The captain of a team can declare his inning over in the event of rain. He thus forces the opposing team to go to bat on wet ground, catching them on a "sticky wicket."

*Reading Time*_____ *Comprehension Score*_____ *Words per Minute*_____   27

Recalling Facts

1. Association football is very much like American
   - ☐ a. soccer.
   - ☐ b. baseball.
   - ☐ c. football.

2. How far apart are the wickets in cricket?
   - ☐ a. 5 yards
   - ☐ b. 16 yards
   - ☐ c. 22 yards

3. A wicket is described as
   - ☐ a. a small basket.
   - ☐ b. several poles.
   - ☐ c. a thick post.

4. Bails look very much like
   - ☐ a. baseballs.
   - ☐ b. pegs.
   - ☐ c. cups.

5. How many players are on a cricket team?
   - ☐ a. six
   - ☐ b. nine
   - ☐ c. eleven

Understanding the Passage

6. Cricket is like a combination of baseball and
   - ☐ a. football.
   - ☐ b. tennis.
   - ☐ c. bowling.

7. A good batter in cricket
   - ☐ a. makes as many runs as he can.
   - ☐ b. stays at bat as long as he can.
   - ☐ c. tries to hit as many fly balls as he can.

8. A "sticky wicket" describes a
   - ☐ a. wet playing field.
   - ☐ b. difficult play.
   - ☐ c. dirty bat.

9. The most serious injuries probably occur in
   - ☐ a. rugby football.
   - ☐ b. association football.
   - ☐ c. cricket.

10. This article is primarily about the most
   - ☐ a. popular sport in Britain.
   - ☐ b. dangerous sport in Britain.
   - ☐ c. complicated sport in Britain.

Look Around You

The environment is everything about you. It can be living, like a forest. It can be non-living, like a rock or a mountain. An environment can be natural or man-made.

There are many kinds of environments. There are cities, small towns, and farms. There are oceans, lakes, deserts, and forests. Each of these has its own mixture of living things and non-living things. Even man-made environments, such as cities, have both living and non-living things. An environment may have such living things as birds, fish, and plants. It has such non-living things as air, soil, and water.

Many animals and plants are found in only one kind of environment. Man, however, can be found in almost all environments. He can even visit places where he needs special equipment to breathe with, such as the moon.

No living thing can live alone. Every living thing depends upon other things in its environment. When something changes, it has an effect on something else. If a non-living thing like water becomes hard to find, plants will be affected. If plants die out, the animals who eat plants will be affected.

Weather, such as temperature, wind, and rain, can change an environment. People can change an environment, too. Some things that people do cause no change or only a small change in the environment. For instance, people can walk through the woods and just observe. People can cut down only a few trees from a large area and still not change the environment very much.

On the other hand, some things that people do cause a lot of change. They can change a whole environment by cutting down a forest.

Not all changes are bad. If we cut down a forest to build houses, plant crops, or make paper, this may not be bad. But what if we cut down all trees in all forests to do these things? What if we didn't save some and replace others? What effect would this have on other living and non-living things in our environment?

It is clear that people have the power to change an environment. What they do has an effect on all the living and non-living things there. This is why it is important to think about the changes before we make them. When people make wise choices, the environment stays healthy. Let's all work together to keep it clean and healthy.

Recalling Facts

1. Which of the following is non-living?
   - ☑ a. air
   - ☐ b. fish
   - ☐ c. plants

2. Which environment is man-made?
   - ☑ a. cities
   - ☐ b. deserts
   - ☐ c. forests

3. If water becomes hard to find, which of the following is first affected?
   - ☐ a. buildings
   - ☑ b. plants
   - ☐ c. rocks

4. A whole environment can be changed by
   - ☑ a. cutting down a forest.
   - ☐ b. painting a country scene.
   - ☐ c. walking through the woods.

5. Before we change anything in an environment, we should
   - ☐ a. ignore any changes.
   - ☐ b. kill all living things.
   - ☑ c. think about the changes.

Understanding the Passage

6. Choose the best title for this article.
   - ☑ a. The Environment and You
   - ☐ b. Pollution is Everywhere
   - ☐ c. Water and Air to Clean

7. This article hints that man
   - ☑ a. can travel from one environment to another.
   - ☐ b. does not enjoy living on the planet Earth.
   - ☐ c. ignores the non-living environments around us.

8. Man cannot live on the moon unless he has special
   - ☑ a. equipment.
   - ☐ b. friends.
   - ☐ c. weapons.

9. We can see that an environment can easily be destroyed by
   - ☐ a. disease.
   - ☑ b. man.
   - ☐ c. nature.

10. In order to save the environment for our future needs, we must
    - ☐ a. destroy all non-living things.
    - ☑ b. keep our environment healthy.
    - ☐ c. kill all animals of prey.

Escaping a fire is a serious matter. Knowing what to do before a fire breaks out can save a life. For example, people should know the safety measures to take before opening a hall door during a fire. Also, make sure everyone knows how to unlock doors that may be in the escape path. At times, a key is needed to unlock a door from the inside. So, keep the key in the lock. Or, you can put the key on a key ring and put it where it can be found easily.

If you live in an apartment, know the ways you can use to get out. Show everyone in the family these routes. Stress the importance of using stairways or fire escapes, not elevators.

From most homes and the lower floors of apartment buildings, escape through windows is possible. Learn the best way of leaving by a window with the least chance of serious injury.

In a home fire, windows are often the only means of escape. The second floor windowsill is usually not more than 13 feet from the ground. An average person, hanging by the fingertips, will have a drop of about six feet to the ground. Of course, it is safer to jump a short way than to stay in a burning building. Roll away from the building when you land.

Windows are also useful when you're waiting for help. Often you'll be able to stay in the room for several minutes if you keep the door closed and the window open. Keep your head low in the window to be sure you get fresh air rather than smoke that may have leaked into the room.

On a second or third floor, the best windows for escape are those which open onto a roof or balcony. From the roof or balcony, a person can either drop to the ground or await rescue. Dropping onto cement or pavement might end in injury. Bushes, soft earth, and grass can help to break a fall. A rope ladder should be considered when the drop is too great.

In a town where the fire department acts quickly, it may be best to wait for rescue. Close the doors and wait by an open window for help. Shout for help. Be sure to close the door before opening a window. Otherwise, smoke and fire may be drawn into the room by the draft.

Recalling Facts

1. Which of the following should not be used when trying to escape a fire?
   - ☐ a. elevators
   - ☐ b. fire escapes
   - ☐ c. stairways

2. From most homes you can escape a fire through the
   - ☐ a. attic.
   - ☐ b. garage.
   - ☐ c. windows.

3. How far from the ground is the second floor windowsill?
   - ☐ a. 13 feet
   - ☐ b. 25 feet
   - ☐ c. 32 feet

4. Often, a second floor window opens onto a porch roof or
   - ☐ a. balcony.
   - ☐ b. driveway.
   - ☐ c. patio.

5. Which of the following helps to break a fall from a second floor window?
   - ☐ a. cement
   - ☐ b. grass
   - ☐ c. pavement

Understanding the Passage

6. This article tells us how to
   - ☐ a. escape a fire.
   - ☐ b. put out a fire.
   - ☐ c. start a fire.

7. This article hints that windows are
   - ☐ a. easily broken.
   - ☐ b. good escape routes.
   - ☐ c. often hard to open.

8. If you are trapped in a room during a fire, it's a good idea to
   - ☐ a. lie under the bed.
   - ☐ b. open a window.
   - ☐ c. stand perfectly still.

9. We can see from this article that
   - ☐ a. breathing in smoke might be harmful.
   - ☐ b. rope ladders should not be used in a fire.
   - ☐ c. youngsters often start most home fires.

10. What is the main idea of this article?
   - ☐ a. Firemen are not well paid or well trained.
   - ☐ b. It is not a good idea to smoke in bed or on a couch.
   - ☐ c. People should know what to do before a fire breaks out.

10   Glancing at Glaciers

Most people have never seen a glacier. Most would say that very few exist. Some folks think glaciers are found only in far-off mountains. Are they really so rare? Think about these facts.

About three-fourths of all the fresh water in the world is stored as glacier ice. This is about the same as 60 years of rainfall all over the globe. In North America there is more water stored as snow and ice in glaciers than in all our lakes, ponds, rivers, and reservoirs.

What is a glacier? Any large mass of snow and ice on land, which lasts for many years, may be called a glacier. Glaciers form when more snow falls than melts over a number of years. The snow packs down and becomes thick. As it is pressed down, it changes into solid ice. Eventually this mass of snow and ice gets very heavy. When this happens it starts to move. If the glacier forms on a slope, it moves downhill. If the glacier is on a flat area, it moves out in all directions.

Glaciers can take several forms. Some are found in shells that are carved out of mountains by the ice itself. Others are found in ridges where much snow is carried by wind drift. Several large valley glaciers join at the foot of a mountain range in Alaska. Large glaciers are also found in Greenland and Antarctica. These are similar in size to the ice sheets that covered much of North America during the Ice Age.

About 3 percent of Alaska is covered by glaciers. These are mostly in mountains not far from the big cities. Most of the large rivers start with these glaciers. The runoff of water from the glaciers affects life in Alaska. These glaciers are an important water source to Alaska. The water is stored in the glaciers during the winter. In winter the need for water is not so great. In the heat of the summer, when the need is greatest, the water melts.

Where can you go to find the best glaciers? To see them in all their varied shapes and sizes, you should travel to Alaska. Air routes fly over or very near some of the largest glaciers in North America. In the United States south of Alaska, the best places to see glaciers are in Mount Rainier National Park.

Recalling Facts

1. Some people think that glaciers are only found in far-off
   - ☐ a. deserts.
   - ☐ b. mountains.
   - ☐ c. prairies.

2. Glaciers are a possible source of
   - ☐ a. food.
   - ☐ b. salt.
   - ☐ c. water.

3. A glacier is a large mass of
   - ☐ a. plants and trees.
   - ☐ b. rocks and soil.
   - ☐ c. snow and ice.

4. Several large valley glaciers are found in
   - ☐ a. Alaska.
   - ☐ b. Hawaii.
   - ☐ c. Texas.

5. Large glaciers are also found in
   - ☐ a. Australia.
   - ☐ b. Bermuda.
   - ☐ c. Greenland.

Understanding the Passage

6. Choose the best title for this article.
   - ☐ a. Antarctica, Here We Come
   - ☐ b. The Great Ice Age
   - ☐ c. What Is a Glacier?

7. This article hints that glaciers are
   - ☐ a. large.
   - ☐ b. poisonous.
   - ☐ c. unimportant.

8. We can guess that glaciers move
   - ☐ a. rapidly.
   - ☐ b. slowly.
   - ☐ c. unevenly.

9. Glaciers are found in
   - ☐ a. cold areas.
   - ☐ b. hot areas.
   - ☐ c. rainy areas.

10. This article suggests that North America was once
    - ☐ a. covered with ice.
    - ☐ b. hot and wet.
    - ☐ c. under water.

11   Beware the Air

Can you see stars at night where you live? If not, the air may be polluted. Polluted air can smell bad or look smoky. But pollution could also be there without your smelling or seeing it.

Air pollution comes from soot, fly ash, and chemicals. These are released by auto exhaust, chimney smoke, burning garbage dumps, and substances sprayed in the air. Soot from burning fuel oil is the main pollutant that gives smoke its dark color. Fly ash is tiny ashes that go up and out of chimneys. They make smoke even darker. Chemicals of many kinds that you cannot see mix with the smoke. Smog, the eye-stinging haze that hangs ● over most cities, is produced when chemicals in the air mix with sunlight.

Air pollutants, such as soot and fly ash, settle down on things and make them dirty. Blown by the wind, air pollutants act like sandpaper and scratch away buildings and statues. Chemical air pollutants discolor and eat away materials. Can you find any change in the color of bricks on old buildings near where you live? Is there a statue in the park that is crumbling away? If you find these things, chances are that air pollution ● was one of the causes.

Plants are also harmed by air pollution. Their leaves may get dry. Brown spots may appear on them. Or the leaves may turn yellow and fall off. Orange and other citrus trees are especially hurt. Even house plants suffer from air pollution from cooking fumes.

Animals are also affected by air pollution. Cattle can get sick, and so can pets. For example, a small amount of some chemicals sprayed near an aquarium may kill pet fish. Care must be taken so that you and your pets are safe from fumes. Harmful fumes can come from many places. ● Fumes from paints, lotions, glue, cleaning fluids, and other chemicals can be harmful.

Even a little air pollution can make your eyes burn and your head ache. It can tire you out. It can blur your vision and make you dizzy. It can also make it hard for you to breathe. Air pollutants can also affect people with asthma. It can make catching colds and flu more likely. Air pollutants have even been linked to some cases of serious diseases, such as lung cancer and heart ailments, thus making air pollution an evil to beware of.

Recalling Facts

1. Air pollution comes from soot, fly ash, and
   - ☐ a. chemicals.
   - ☐ b. litter.
   - ☐ c. sunlight.

2. What gives smoke its dark color?
   - ☐ a. charcoal
   - ☐ b. pollen
   - ☐ c. soot

3. Tiny ashes that go up and out the chimney are called
   - ☐ a. fly ash.
   - ☐ b. fly aways.
   - ☐ c. fly soot.

4. The eye-stinging haze that hangs over most cities is called
   - ☐ a. ash.
   - ☐ b. fog.
   - ☐ c. smog.

5. Materials can be eaten away and discolored by
   - ☐ a. chemical air pollutants.
   - ☐ b. cooking grease.
   - ☐ c. untreated sewage.

Understanding the Passage

6. Polluted air
   - ☐ a. helps to put out fires.
   - ☐ b. may not smell bad.
   - ☐ c. is good for plants.

7. Which of the following causes air pollution?
   - ☐ a. automobiles
   - ☐ b. plants
   - ☐ c. sunlight

8. Chemical air pollutants can
   - ☐ a. destroy buildings.
   - ☐ b. help people with asthma.
   - ☐ c. make plants grow.

9. Cooking fumes can be harmful to
   - ☐ a. house plants.
   - ☐ b. nearby neighbors.
   - ☐ c. small infants.

10. We can see that air pollution
   - ☐ a. can make you sick.
   - ☐ b. is not very common.
   - ☐ c. may help cure the common cold.

An Indian Hero

Black Hawk was a Sauk Indian who hated the white settlers. For years, the Sauk and Fox Indians had hunted and fished in what is now Illinois and Wisconsin. Then white settlers pushed into the area. Under an unfair treaty, the settlers took the land.

From boyhood Black Hawk learned to hate the white man. His fame as a fearless warrior began at age 15 when he killed and scalped his first man. He went on to fight enemy Indian tribes. Later, he fought the white man.

Above all, Black Hawk hated the 1804 treaty which had taken away Sauk and Fox lands. He spoke against the treaty. He called it unfair since the Indians who had signed it were tricked into agreeing to its terms. Black Hawk believed that Indian land could not be sold. He was determined to stay and farm the land.

Black Hawk and his followers refused to leave their villages. By 1831, the Indians found themselves unable to farm their own lands. Black Hawk ordered the whites to get out or be killed. Instead, soldiers moved in and threw the Indians off the land.

Black Hawk felt that he could band enough Indians together to fight the white man. He set out to ask other tribes for help. In April 1832, Black Hawk and several hundred warriors returned to Illinois. He was ready to drive the whites from Indian land. The fighting known as "Black Hawk's War" began. Soon troops from Washington were sent into the field to put down the Indians. For three months the Indians managed to escape the troops. They won several small battles and were raiding the Illinois frontier.

The tide turned as more soldiers poured in. The troops chased the Indians from Illinois to Mississippi. There, Black Hawk was trapped. He faced the steamship Warrior on one side and the army on the other. His band was nearly destroyed. The Sauk leader escaped to a Winnebago village. There he gave himself up and was taken to a prison camp in chains. A few months later he was freed.

In 1838, at the age of 71, Black Hawk died in his lodge on the Des Moines River. He had ordered that his body be seated on the ground beneath a wooden shelter. The Indians' faith in this Sauk tradition attests to an undying belief in their culture.

Recalling Facts

1. Black Hawk was a
   - ☐ a. Fox Indian.
   - ☐ b. Sauk Indian.
   - ☐ c. Sioux Indian.

2. Black Hawk's fame as a warrior began when he was
   - ☐ a. 10.
   - ☐ b. 15.
   - ☐ c. 20.

3. Black Hawk
   - ☐ a. hated the 1804 treaty.
   - ☐ b. liked the 1804 treaty.
   - ☐ c. signed the 1804 treaty.

4. The soldiers chased Black Hawk from Illinois to
   - ☐ a. Florida.
   - ☐ b. Mississippi.
   - ☐ c. Texas.

5. Black Hawk died at the age of
   - ☐ a. 65.
   - ☐ b. 71.
   - ☐ c. 82.

Understanding the Passage

6. Black Hawk lived in
   - ☐ a. New England.
   - ☐ b. the Midwest.
   - ☐ c. the deep South.

7. We can see that at times
   - ☐ a. the Indians grew tasty corn.
   - ☐ b. Indian tribes fought each other.
   - ☐ c. white settlers traveled in wagons.

8. This article hints that the white man treated the Indians
   - ☐ a. kindly.
   - ☐ b. respectfully.
   - ☐ c. unfairly.

9. The Sauk Indians were mostly
   - ☐ a. farmers.
   - ☐ b. fishermen.
   - ☐ c. hunters.

10. How long did it take Black Hawk to gather his Indian warriors?
   - ☐ a. one year
   - ☐ b. two years
   - ☐ c. three years

A Smart Shopper

Where you do your food shopping often affects your grocery bill. It's best to check the prices in nearby stores for the foods you buy all the time. You can then decide which store gives you the best prices. Check, too, for other features that may be useful to you. Which store offers the freshest foods? Which store has off-street parking and will cash your checks?

Small stores often will deliver orders to your home. If you do not need this service, you will do better shopping at a large chain. The large chain markets offer more variety and have better prices.

For most people it is best to choose a store with good prices and stay with it. Store-hopping for sales on certain foods may save you pennies, but it can be costly in time and gas.

When you shop depends on your schedule. Try to go when the store is not too crowded and when you have time to choose with care. Study labels and compare prices. Learn about new products. Give food buying all the attention it deserves.

The meat, poultry, and fish items in your menu usually cost the most. Studies show that one-third of the money spent on food goes for these items. To take advantage of the best buys at the meat counter, you need to be aware of the many cuts of meat that are available. Also, you must know how to use them in meals. Keep in mind that the economy of a cut depends on the amount of cooked lean meat it serves as well as its price per pound. Often the cut with a low price per pound is not the best buy. What counts is the amount of lean meat and the number of servings it will provide. For example, a high-priced meat with little or no waste may be a better buy than a low-priced cut with a great deal of bone or fat.

Same-size servings of cooked lean meat from different types and cuts of meat often have the same food value. As a rule, cooked lean meat from pot roast is as nutritious as that from steak. Fish has as much nutrition as lamb, and turkey has as much as veal. So when you visit the market, be a smart shopper and take time to make the right choice.

---

*Reading Time*_____ *Comprehension Score*_____ *Words per Minute*_____

Recalling Facts

1. For foods you buy all the time, it is good to check different stores to find the best
   □ a. cashiers.
   □ b. prices.
   □ c. registers.

2. Store-hopping wastes
   □ a. groceries.
   □ b. clothes.
   □ c. time.

3. When choosing a product carefully, you should look at the price and the
   □ a. cashiers.
   □ b. carriage.
   □ c. label.

4. One-third of the grocery bill is spent on
   □ a. cheese, milk, and eggs.
   □ b. meat, poultry, and fish.
   □ c. vegetables and fruits.

5. Cooked lean pot roast is just as nutritious as
   □ a. potatoes.
   □ b. steak.
   □ c. sugar.

Understanding the Passage

6. Large chain markets do *not*
   □ a. have a large variety of foods.
   □ b. offer the freshest foods.
   □ c. make home grocery deliveries.

7. We can see that store-hopping
   □ a. is often the sign of a wise shopper.
   □ b. may cost you more money than it saves.
   □ c. will cut down on your grocery bill.

8. This article hints that meat
   □ a. is expensive.
   □ b. is not nutritious.
   □ c. spoils easily.

9. A cheap cut of meat may not be as good a buy as a
   □ a. heavily salted cut.
   □ b. more expensive cut.
   □ c. well-packaged cut.

10. What is the main idea of this article?
    □ a. Careful food shopping can save you money.
    □ b. Large food markets have small parking lots.
    □ c. Small food stores are very scarce.

14   Lost in the Woods

If you get lost in the woods, a little knowledge can turn what some people call a hardship into an enjoyable stay away from the woes of modern society. Many high-pressured businesspeople would willingly get themselves lost in the outdoors for several days if they only knew how enjoyable it can be with a minimum of know-how.

When you think you are lost, sit down on a log or a rock or lean against a tree and recite something that you have memorized to bring your mind to a point where it is under control.

Don't run wildly helter-skelter! If you must move, don't follow streams unless you know the stream, and in that case you are not lost. Streams normally flow through swampland before they reach a lake or a river. Though there are more edible plants per square inch in a swamp, there may also be quicksand, poisonous snakes, and other hazards.

Many experts feel that it is wisest to walk uphill. At the top of most hills and mountains are trails leading back to civilization. If there are no trails, you are much easier to find on top of a hill, and you may even spot a highway or a railroad from this vantage point.

Nowadays, the first way someone will look for you is by air. In a swamp or in dense growth you are very hard to spot.

Any time that you go into the woods, somebody should know where you are going and when you expect to return. Also, when someone comes looking, you should be able to signal to them.

The best way that you can signal in the daytime is with a good smoky fire. In most of our country either a fire tower or airplane will quickly spot the smoke. A fire warden will come to your rescue. At night, a bright fire will bring help if someone knows you are lost.

In the old days whenever you got lost, you could fire your weapon three times. Today lots of hunters fire a half dozen shots without hitting game. However, if you save your shots until after dark and fire one shot, then wait for a half hour or so and fire another, in less time than it takes to get your third shot off a game warden or a ranger should be there to show you the way out of the woods.

Recalling Facts

1. If a person becomes lost and wants to walk, he should move
   ☐ a. uphill.
   ☐ b. downhill.
   ☐ c. northerly.

2. Nowadays, the first way someone will look for you is by
   ☐ a. vehicle.
   ☐ b. foot.
   ☐ c. plane.

3. The best way to signal for help, night or day, is with
   ☐ a. a mirror.
   ☐ b. broken branches.
   ☐ c. a fire.

4. Years ago, a signal for help meant firing a weapon how many times?
   ☐ a. two
   ☐ b. three
   ☐ c. four

5. The kinds of plants found in swamps are usually
   ☐ a. deceptive.
   ☐ b. edible.
   ☐ c. poisonous.

Understanding the Passage

6. In swamps and dense growth, a person is
   ☐ a. hard to find.
   ☐ b. much safer.
   ☐ c. quite visible.

7. If you become lost, the first action the author advises is
   ☐ a. searching immediately for help.
   ☐ b. retracing your steps into the woods.
   ☐ c. sitting down and getting control of yourself.

8. Following a stream may
   ☐ a. allow you to find your way out.
   ☐ b. take you deeper into unknown territory.
   ☐ c. expose you to unexpected dangers.

9. The author implies that becoming lost should not be
   ☐ a. pleasurable.
   ☐ b. frightening.
   ☐ c. enlightening.

10. The author of this selection wishes to be
    ☐ a. instructive.
    ☐ b. controversial.
    ☐ c. scientific.

15   Moving Along with the Times

Moving from one home to another can be a problem. If your new house is empty, it may seem as cold and as lifeless as a tomb. However, little by little, you get settled. Your furniture arrives. Your clothes fill the closets. Before you know it, you look around and realize that all is in order. Moving wasn't so bad after all.

As a matter of fact, most people seem to enjoy it. Moving is one of the most widely shared adventures of our way of life. Long before the pioneers headed for the West, restlessness had been part of our nature. Today, it shows itself up and down and across the land as 40 million Americans change their homes every year.

Today, those who make long distance moves usually fall into one of three classes. Some are skilled workers who are seeking better jobs. Others are in military or government service and have been assigned to new posts.

The third class of mover shows the changing pattern of business life. About four out of ten long-distance moves are the result of job transfers. These are usually young businesspeople who are often moved from one office to another. Some businesspeople move as often as every two years.

Today, a long distance move need not be unpleasant. Just be sure you plan well. In fact, it could be nothing more than a short break in the daily routine. Moving companies now have trained people with years of experience. They know how to ship all kinds of things. They can even handle fine art and antiques. Valuable instruments can be shipped without a scratch.

Damage to household goods in packing or on route is no longer a real problem. New ways for crating, packing, and shipping have been found. For instance, some movers now use self-adjusting cartons for things like china and glasses. These cartons keep your glassware safe. Also, some companies use stuffing and plastic wrapping materials to protect delicate items.

On the way, the shipment is in the hands of drivers who are considered the best in the world today. The drivers of household moving vans are selected as the cream of the crop. They travel an average of 60,000 to 100,000 miles a year. That's a lot of miles. And it's a lot of experience. Moving is not so bad when you know you have skilled movers to help you.

Recalling Facts

1. How many Americans change their homes each year?
   - ☐ a. 10 million
   - ☐ b. 20 million
   - ☐ c. 40 million

2. Skilled workers often move to find better
   - ☐ a. weather.
   - ☐ b. jobs.
   - ☐ c. schools.

3. About four out of ten long-distance moves are the result of
   - ☐ a. larger families.
   - ☐ b. poor health.
   - ☐ c. job transfers.

4. Which of the following is used to protect glassware items?
   - ☐ a. metal racks
   - ☐ b. self-adjusting cartons
   - ☐ c. sturdy wooden crates

5. The drivers of household vans are carefully
   - ☐ a. educated.
   - ☐ b. tested.
   - ☐ c. selected.

Understanding the Passage

6. An empty house may seem
   - ☐ a. lifelike.
   - ☐ b. lifeless.
   - ☐ c. lively.

7. This article hints that a lot of people
   - ☐ a. hate to move.
   - ☐ b. like to move.
   - ☐ c. never move.

8. Young businesspeople seem to
   - ☐ a. be well schooled.
   - ☐ b. have large families.
   - ☐ c. move a lot.

9. We can see that
   - ☐ a. a well-planned move is not unpleasant.
   - ☐ b. moving from one place to another is difficult.
   - ☐ c. movers make a good salary each year.

10. Foam stuffing helps to protect your delicate items from
    - ☐ a. breaking.
    - ☐ b. freezing.
    - ☐ c. melting.

Many pests that invade homes are present at all times in all parts of the United States. Some are found only at certain times or in certain areas.

Many kinds of ants invade homes. Some ants have wings. Termites quickly shed their wings soon after they enter a building. Thus, ants are often mistaken for termites.

The two insects, however, are very different in appearance. Ants are "pinched in" at the waistline. Termites have no "pinching in" at the waistline. Also, the rear wings of an ant are much smaller than the front wings. But there is little difference in size between the rear and front wings of a termite.

Ants crawl over any food they can reach. They spoil it for humans and carry bits of it to their nests.

Ants usually do not attack fabrics, leather, or similar materials found in homes. They seldom attack very sound wood as termites do, but some kinds damage old wooden structures. They make their nests in the rotting woodwork.

The ants' nest may be outdoors or it may be within a wall in the house. The nest may be under flooring, under a pile of papers, or in an out-of-the-way corner. Sometimes it is possible to trace the ants' line of march from the food source to the location of the nest.

If the nest is found, it should be treated with insecticide. If the nest is outdoors, all cracks and openings into the house through which the ants might enter should be sealed off.

For most places, an insecticide can be applied as a surface spray. For kitchen treatments, the liquid can be applied with a small paintbrush.

Insecticide must be applied to surfaces over which the ants crawl in their line of march. All cracks, openings, or runways that they may be using to enter the house must be treated. These may include the lower part of window frames; around doors, supports, posts, pillars, or pipes that the ants might use as runways into the house; cracks in baseboards, walls, and floors; and openings around electrical outlets and plumbing or heating pipes.

It will take a few days for the ants to reach the insecticide deposits. If the pests continue to appear, they probably are using surfaces that have not been treated. Those surfaces must then be found and treated.

Recalling Facts

1. Termites shed their wings
   soon after they
   ☐ a. become adults.
   ☐ b. breed.
   ☐ c. enter a building.

2. Ants usually do not eat
   or destroy
   ☐ a. wood.
   ☐ b. leather.
   ☐ c. garbage.

3. Insecticides are used to
   ☐ a. protect food.
   ☐ b. kill bugs.
   ☐ c. seal cracks.

4. Insects often enter the
   living quarters of a house
   ☐ a. on clothes.
   ☐ b. in groceries.
   ☐ c. through electrical boxes.

5. The rear wings of ants are
   ☐ a. larger than the
       front wings.
   ☐ b. smaller than the
       front wings.
   ☐ c. often the same size as
       the front wings.

Understanding the Passage

6. According to the author,
   ants are
   ☐ a. members of the
       termite family.
   ☐ b. really a kind of termite.
   ☐ c. often mistaken for termites.

7. The article suggests that termites
   ☐ a. are more destructive
       than ants.
   ☐ b. often carry food from
       the kitchen area.
   ☐ c. are much larger than ants.

8. In this article, the author is
   concerned primarily with
   ☐ a. protection from ants.
   ☐ b. the habits of termites.
   ☐ c. the use of pesticides.

9. The author states that
   ☐ a. ants sometimes build
       their nests outside.
   ☐ b. termites breed more
       rapidly than ants.
   ☐ c. termites make tunnels in
       the wood they attack.

10. The reader can conclude that
    ☐ a. insects are man's greatest
        natural enemy.
    ☐ b. insect damage is often
        more obvious than the
        insects themselves.
    ☐ c. insects are usually afraid
        of sunlight.

In the Caribbean

The Caribbean islands are divided into two worlds: a rich one and a poor one.

This tropical region's economy is based mainly on farming. Farmers are of two types. One is the plantation owner, who may have hundreds of thousands of acres. In contrast, the small cultivator is working only a few acres of land. Most visitors to the Caribbean are rich, like the plantation owner. They do not realize, or do not want to realize, that many farm families barely manage to get by on what they grow.

The Caribbean produces many things. Sugar is the main product. Other export crops are tobacco, coffee, bananas, citrus fruits, and spices. From the West Indies also come oil, asphalt, and many forest products. Jamaica's aluminum ore supplies are the world's largest. Oil comes from Trinidad, Aruba, and Curacao. But for many of the smaller islands, sugar is the only export.

Rum, which is distilled from sugar cane, is also an export. The world's best rum comes from this area. Local kinds vary from the light rums of Puerto Rico to the heavier, darker rums of Barbados and Jamaica. American tourists enjoy stocking up on inexpensive, high quality Caribbean rum while they are on vacation. In Curacao, the well-known liquor of that name is made from the rinds of a native orange.

Ever since America's colonial days, the Caribbean islands have been favorite places to visit. Since World War II tourism has increased rapidly. Because great numbers of people go there, the islanders have built elaborate resorts, developed harbors and airfields, improved beaches, and have expanded sea and air routes. Everything is at the resort: hotel, beach, shopping, recreation. The vacationer never has any reason to explore the island.

As in most places, those who have money live well indeed. Those who don't have money live at various levels of poverty. But here, the poor greatly outnumber the wealthy.

A visitor will find rich people living in Spanish villas or apartments. Their servants might include a cook, a maid, and a nurse for the children.

Most of the people live well below the poverty level. In towns, they live crowded together in tiny houses. Islanders make the best they can of what they have. Their homes are much less ornate than condominiums or hotel resorts. Sadly, most tourists never see this side of the Caribbean.

Recalling Facts

1. The Caribbean islands are
   ☐ a. temperate.
   ☐ b. semi-tropical.
   ☐ c. tropical.

2. The economy of the Caribbean islands is based on
   ☐ a. tourism.
   ☐ b. industry.
   ☐ c. farming.

3. Jamaica is the world's largest supplier of
   ☐ a. sugar.
   ☐ b. aluminum.
   ☐ c. tobacco.

4. Sugar cane can be distilled into
   ☐ a. rum.
   ☐ b. vinegar.
   ☐ c. cooking oil.

5. Most people on the islands are
   ☐ a. wealthy.
   ☐ b. middle class.
   ☐ c. poor.

Understanding the Passage

6. This article is primarily about
   ☐ a. industry in the West Indies.
   ☐ b. vacationing in the Caribbean.
   ☐ c. the economy of Caribbean islands.

7. The article states that
   ☐ a. even rich people in the West Indies cannot afford servants.
   ☐ b. farm land is owned by the government.
   ☐ c. several varieties of rum are made in the Caribbean.

8. We can conclude that sugar cane grows well in
   ☐ a. a tropical climate.
   ☐ b. an arid climate.
   ☐ c. a cool climate.

9. Ever since America's colonial days, the
   ☐ a. islands have been United States colonies.
   ☐ b. Caribbean islands have welcomed tourists.
   ☐ c. islands have wanted to become states.

10. The island of Curacao is famous for its
    ☐ a. wide, sandy beaches.
    ☐ b. beautiful gardens.
    ☐ c. orange-flavored liquor.

18   Delightful Diving Ducks

Have you ever heard of a diving duck? Believe it or not, there is such a creature. As the name suggests, these ducks normally dive for their food. When they dive, they find the plant and animal food they need.

Sometimes these birds feed at great depths. They feed in wetlands, lakes, bays, and streams. You won't find the diver looking for its food on land. The ones you do see are the more common puddle ducks like the mallard or the pintail.

As you might guess, diving ducks depend upon the water. They have short legs and large feet located far back on their bodies. This causes them to look clumsy on land. They use a running type takeoff and a skidding type landing. Divers tend to gather in large numbers on the open water of lakes. The flocks often move from place to place looking for good feeding spots. Many kinds of divers use the same feeding grounds year after year.

In early March, diving ducks migrate. They leave the coastal waters and head north to their breeding grounds. Most ducks are already paired. Courtship continues along the route. The flight ends at the nesting grounds where the female lays its eggs. Most diving duck hens lay from 7 to 12 eggs and sit on them for about 4 weeks. The new ducklings are able to swim and to find their own food soon after hatching. But they depend upon the hen for safety.

Water, of course, is of great importance to the ducklings. This is their only source of food and cover. Nearly all water plants provide both food and cover. Most shallow ponds and marshes are filled with tiny insects that the ducklings eat.

Waterfowl lose their wing feathers in the summer. At this time they can't fly. This is called the annual molt. At this time, their movement is limited. This is when they are easy prey for their enemies. During the molting time, the birds need large wetlands. These wetlands have food, cover and water. They give the helpless fowl a safe shelter.

But man has caused many problems for waterfowl. There is much to be learned about the best ways to keep and improve wetlands. The draining of wetlands has been a curse to diving ducks and other wildlife in general. Just being able to see and enjoy wild waterfowl may become a thing of the past.

---

*Reading Time*_____ *Comprehension Score*_____ *Words per Minute*_____

Recalling Facts

1. Diving ducks dive to get
   - ☐ a. a drink.
   - ☐ b. food.
   - ☐ c. a mate.

2. One type of puddle duck is the
   - ☐ a. eider.
   - ☐ b. mallard.
   - ☐ c. wood duck.

3. Diving ducks have
   - ☐ a. big eyes.
   - ☐ b. large feet.
   - ☐ c. long feathers.

4. When do diving ducks migrate?
   - ☐ a. March
   - ☐ b. April
   - ☐ c. May

5. A diving duck hen sits on her eggs for about
   - ☐ a. 2 weeks.
   - ☐ b. 4 weeks.
   - ☐ c. 6 weeks.

Understanding the Passage

6. Where would you most likely find a diving duck's nest?
   - ☐ a. in a cave
   - ☐ b. near a pond
   - ☐ c. on top of a mountain

7. The pintail looks for its food
   - ☐ a. in the air.
   - ☐ b. in lakes.
   - ☐ c. on land.

8. We can see that diving ducks
   - ☐ a. are easy to hunt.
   - ☐ b. live in groups.
   - ☐ c. never get wet.

9. Female diving ducks lay their eggs
   - ☐ a. before they migrate north.
   - ☐ b. after they migrate north.
   - ☐ c. as they migrate north.

10. Diving duck hens
    - ☐ a. kill their young.
    - ☐ b. leave their young alone.
    - ☐ c. protect their young.

Up, Up, and Away

It was late in September 1903 when the Wright brothers reached their camp at Kill Devil Hills. There were delays caused by problems with their machine. There were more delays caused by bad weather. At last, on December 14, they were ready to fly their machine.

The first trial was not successful. There was not enough wind to start from level ground, so they took their machine to the slope of a hill. The plane was placed on a special track they had built and was ready to go. Wilbur won the toss of a coin. He was to have the first try. When *The Flyer* left the track, but before it had gained enough speed, Wilbur turned it upward too suddenly. It climbed a few feet, stalled, and settled to the ground. It came to rest at the foot of the hill after just 3½ seconds in the air. Parts of the track had broken. Two more days were needed for repairs.

On the morning of December 17, the wind was blowing up to 27 miles an hour. Hoping it would die down, the Wrights waited. When the wind kept up, they decided to go ahead anyway and attempt a flight. They picked a smooth stretch of level ground just west of the camp. The track was laid and pointed into the wind. It was now Orville's turn.

Orville nestled himself into the control mechanism on the lower wing. The machine started down the track traveling slowly into the 27-mile-an-hour wind. After running 40 feet on the track, the plane took off. It climbed 10 feet into the air, dipped up and down several times, and dropped to earth about 120 feet from the takeoff point. The flight lasted only 12 seconds. Nevertheless, it was the first flight in history.

The brothers took turns making three more flights that morning. Each flight became longer than the one before. On the fourth flight, Wilbur flew 852 feet in 59 seconds. It was not possible to correct the up-and-down motion of the machine before it struck the ground. This is why the flights were so short. While the Wrights were discussing the flights with on-lookers, a gust of wind struck the plane. The plane was flipped over and badly damaged. It could not be repaired in time for any more flights that year. In fact, it never flew again.

Recalling Facts

1. The Wright brothers flew
   their machine in
   ☐ a. 1803.
   ☐ b. 1903.
   ☐ c. 1953.

2. The Wright brothers made
   their camp at
   ☐ a. Devil's Canyon.
   ☐ b. Kill Devil Hills.
   ☐ c. Snake River Hill.

3. During the first trial,
   the plane was placed on
   a special
   ☐ a. crane.
   ☐ b. platform.
   ☐ c. track.

4. On the first try, the plane
   stayed in the air
   ☐ a. 3½ seconds.
   ☐ b. 3½ minutes.
   ☐ c. 3½ hours.

5. Orville nestled himself
   into the
   ☐ a. control mechanism.
   ☐ b. flight deck.
   ☐ c. wing span.

Understanding the Passage

6. Choose the best title for
   this article.
   ☐ a. The First Flight
   ☐ b. Many Different Airplanes
   ☐ c. An Unsuccessful Event

7. In order to fly their machine, the
   Wright brothers waited for
   ☐ a. good weather.
   ☐ b. a large crowd.
   ☐ c. news reporters.

8. What was the name of the plane?
   ☐ a. *The Bird*
   ☐ b. *The Flyer*
   ☐ c. *The Gypsy*

9. Who flew the first
   successful flight?
   ☐ a. James
   ☐ b. Orville
   ☐ c. Wilbur

10. This article hints that
    ☐ a. flying an airplane is
       an easy task.
    ☐ b. people came to watch
       the Wright brothers.
    ☐ c. Orville was killed in a
       plane crash.

20   A Friend in Need

The first step in stopping drug abuse is knowing why people start to use drugs. The reasons people abuse drugs are as different as people are from one another. But there seems to be one common thread. People seem to take drugs to change the way they feel. They want to feel better or to feel happy or to feel nothing. Sometimes they want to forget or to remember. To them drugs seem to be the best way to change a mood.

People often feel better about themselves when they are high on drugs, but the effects don't last long. Drugs don't solve problems; they just post- pone them. No matter how far drugs take you, it's always a round trip. After a while people who misuse drugs may feel worse about themselves. This gets them trapped in a spiral of more drug use.

If someone you know is using or abusing drugs, you can help. The most important part you can play is to be there. You can let your friend know that you care. You can listen and try to solve the problem behind your friend's need to use drugs. Two people together can often solve a problem that seems too big for one person alone.

Stopping drug abuse may be as simple as having something better to do than taking drugs. Most cities have centers to go to to talk and relax. Sometimes, there are team sports to join in. If there aren't things like this where you live, you and your friends could start something. It could be sports, a band, arts and crafts, skateboarding, almost anything you have fun doing. All these things can prevent drug abuse.

This might sound too simple or too easy to work. But think about it. Studies of heavy drug users show that they felt unloved and unwanted. They didn't have close friends to talk to. They didn't have friends to have fun with or to share things with. When you or your friends take the time to care for each other, you're all helping to stop drug abuse. You probably know what you'd do if your friend were falling off a mountain. What would you do if he or she were getting involved with drugs? It could be important for you to know what to do. It is your business to help. After all, what are friends for?

Recalling Facts

1. The first step in stopping drug abuse is to find out why people
   - ☐ a. make drugs.
   - ☐ b. sell drugs.
   - ☐ c. use drugs.

2. People use drugs because they want to change their
   - ☐ a. mood.
   - ☐ b. address.
   - ☐ c. looks.

3. The best way to help a friend who is using drugs is to
   - ☐ a. ignore your friend.
   - ☐ b. offer your help.
   - ☐ c. report your friend.

4. One way to stop drug abuse is to get involved in
   - ☐ a. reading.
   - ☐ b. school.
   - ☐ c. sports.

5. Studies show that heavy drug users feel
   - ☐ a. happy and content.
   - ☐ b. satisfied and relaxed.
   - ☐ c. unloved and unwanted.

Understanding the Passage

6. What does this article hint at?
   - ☐ a. Doctors will not prescribe dangerous drugs.
   - ☐ b. Some people enjoy using drugs.
   - ☐ c. There are many reasons why people use drugs.

7. Taking drugs
   - ☐ a. does not harm the body in any way.
   - ☐ b. may cause more problems than it solves.
   - ☐ c. is just a fad and will soon pass.

8. Which of these would be a good title for this article?
   - ☐ a. Read Your Labels
   - ☐ b. Stop Drug Abuse
   - ☐ c. You and Your Community

9. Many people probably take drugs because they are
   - ☐ a. unhappy.
   - ☐ b. unkind.
   - ☐ c. unfaithful.

10. What is the main idea of this passage?
    - ☐ a. Cities have many programs to help drug addicts.
    - ☐ b. Friends can help someone who is using drugs.
    - ☐ c. Society just ignores the drug abuse problem.

21 Gentle Gerbils

Gerbils are small, brown rodents that evolved in the desert regions of Asia. The underside of a gerbil's body is white, and they have long tails. They need little care and make good pets.

Because gerbils might escape, breed quickly, and destroy valuable crops in the desert regions of the West, they should not be taken as pets to western Texas, Arizona, or New Mexico. California has a law making it illegal to take gerbils into that state as pets.

A pet gerbil should be easy to tame. These little animals have a natural curiosity, a gentle nature, and no fear of people. When you lift your gerbil, slide your fingers under its body and hold it firmly in both hands. If necessary, you may lift it by the base of the tail. Never lift it by the end of the tail.

Keep your gerbil in a wooden, metal, or wire cage or a glass aquarium. The cage should be fourteen or more inches square and about a foot deep. Cages and other equipment are available in pet supply stores. Be sure to put the cage in a part of the house that is free of drafts. If your gerbil is in direct sunlight, provide it with shade.

Put a small shelf in one corner of the cage about three inches from the floor. Your gerbil will burrow through its bedding and sleep under the shelf. You may put a small box in the cage instead of a shelf. Keep a block of wood in the cage for your gerbil to gnaw on. If you keep a single gerbil, give it toys.

Use wood shavings, shredded paper, or some other absorbent material on the floor of the cage as bedding. Change the bedding and clean the cage once a week.

A feed box and water bottle should be attached to the side of the cage. Be sure the water spout does not touch the bedding. If it does, the water will run out into the cage.

Keep food and water available at all times. Your gerbil will eat the same kind of food that is eaten by mice, hamsters, or guinea pigs. They like pellets, grain, cereals, and fresh fruit or vegetables.

If you wish to raise young gerbils, you can keep a male and female in the same cage. They mate for life and should be left together all the time.

Recalling Facts

1. Gerbils evolved in
   - ☐ a. Africa.
   - ☐ b. Asia.
   - ☐ c. Europe.

2. Gerbils should not be taken as pets to
   - ☐ a. Alabama.
   - ☐ b. Alaska.
   - ☐ c. Arizona.

3. Which state has a law that makes it illegal to own gerbils?
   - ☐ a. California
   - ☐ b. Maryland
   - ☐ c. Nevada

4. Gerbils are
   - ☐ a. curious.
   - ☐ b. intelligent.
   - ☐ c. timid.

5. Cages in which gerbils are kept should be at least
   - ☐ a. six inches deep.
   - ☐ b. nine inches deep.
   - ☐ c. twelve inches deep.

Understanding the Passage

6. The author implies that
   - ☐ a. drafts are not healthy for gerbils.
   - ☐ b. gerbils should be kept in cool rooms.
   - ☐ c. gerbils do not need water to live.

7. The reader can infer that
   - ☐ a. most gerbils live two years.
   - ☐ b. gerbils have very sharp teeth.
   - ☐ c. some gerbils have gray stripes on their backs.

8. Gerbils can be fed
   - ☐ a. small scraps of meat.
   - ☐ b. pieces of carrots.
   - ☐ c. insects.

9. When baby gerbils are born,
   - ☐ a. the mother and father gerbil should be separated.
   - ☐ b. the baby gerbils should be put in a separate cage.
   - ☐ c. both parent gerbils should remain to care for the young.

10. When gerbils live in nature, they
    - ☐ a. climb trees.
    - ☐ b. like hot, dry areas.
    - ☐ c. eat insects.

A Lively Lake Indeed!

The history of Lake Michigan is a history of ships. The first sailing ship was LaSalle's "Griffin." It was made of wood from the nearby forests. The ship left Detroit in 1670. It carried furs. Sadly, the ship didn't reach its goal. It vanished without a trace. The Indians believed that the ship fell through a crack in the lake.

Many ships have vanished without a trace. Legends tell of underground channels that join one Great Lake to another. Other tales tell of waterspouts that lift ships out of Lake Michigan and put them down in Lake Huron.

A new ship, the whaleback, appeared on the lakes in 1889. Her sides looked like the top half of a whale. Waves easily rolled over it. On her first voyage through Lake Michigan, the whaleback "Charles Wetmore" carried a load of wheat. When the hatches were lifted after a stormy trip, everyone was amazed. The ship had been so steady that the footprint of the cargo trimmer could still be seen on top of the grain.

By the end of the 19th century things changed. A thousand schooners plowed the lake at 16 knots. But schooners did not last. They were replaced by steamers. The changeover from sail to steam was fought by the old-timers. At first, steamers had to have running lights. Schooners did not. Sail ships were given the right of way over steamships. Despite the effort to keep the schooners, they were doomed. Just as the horse and buggy gave way to the automobile, so the schooner gave way to steamships. At last the proud schooners became no more than barges, pulled by tugs.

The early steamships that sailed on Lake Michigan were called "teakettles on a raft." The Indians thought they were pulled by fish. "Independence" was the first Lake Michigan ship to go through the city of Sault St. Marie. Before the canal locks were built, the ship was pulled on greased ways through icy streets. It took a team of horses to move the ship four feet a day.

One early steamer, the "Cayuga," had a steel hull. One night she hit the wooden boat "Hurd" and sank. Flour from the sunken "Cayuga" washed ashore the next day in chunks of dough. The dough began to bake on the hot sand.

Is it any wonder that stories like these are called the Legends of Lake Michigan?

Recalling Facts

1. The first sailing ship on Lake Michigan was LaSalle's
   - [ ] a. "Cayuga."
   - [ ] b. "Griffin."
   - [ ] c. "Hurd."

2. The "Charles Wetmore" carried a load of
   - [ ] a. flour.
   - [ ] b. furs.
   - [ ] c. wheat.

3. The early steamships were called "teakettles on a
   - [ ] a. barge."
   - [ ] b. raft."
   - [ ] c. stove."

4. The "Independence" was pulled through the city of
   - [ ] a. Chicago.
   - [ ] b. Detroit.
   - [ ] c. Sault St. Marie.

5. How many feet a day could the "Independence" be moved?
   - [ ] a. three
   - [ ] b. four
   - [ ] c. five

Understanding the Passage

6. Choose the best title for this article.
   - [ ] a. Great Indian Legends
   - [ ] b. History of Lake Michigan
   - [ ] c. Steamers on the Move

7. This article hints that
   - [ ] a. early steamships traveled slowly.
   - [ ] b. many ships have disappeared on Lake Michigan.
   - [ ] c. Indians often attacked the whalebacks.

8. The Indians around Lake Michigan were
   - [ ] a. fierce.
   - [ ] b. superstitious.
   - [ ] c. warlike.

9. The whaleback ships handled well during a
   - [ ] a. drought.
   - [ ] b. flood.
   - [ ] c. storm.

10. Steamers appeared on Lake Michigan
    - [ ] a. after the schooners.
    - [ ] b. before the schooners.
    - [ ] c. before the whalebacks.

23   Lend an Ear

Noise is ear pollution. It is often called "unwanted sound." If a sound is something you like, a song, or a call from a friend, it is just a sound. But if you are trying to sleep or study, then this sound becomes a noise.

This "unwanted sound" has an effect upon our bodies. For example, loud noises can cause a loss of hearing. Even wanted sound, such as amplified rock-and-roll music, can hurt your hearing, though you may not think of it as noise. The first warning that a sound may be loud enough to hurt is called "ear distress." This would be felt as a pain or heard as a ringing   ●
noise in the ear. People who have this complaint should be examined by a doctor.

Noise of any kind may make you nervous or affect your sleep. Noise can also affect your speech and your ability to think. Noise has been linked to cases of heart disease, ulcers, mental illness, and other sicknesses.

Noise, of course, is not always bad. It does have a place in our lives. You may not like to hear car horns, but they do warn you of oncoming cars when you cross a street. A thumping noise from a bicycle tire tells you   ●
that the tire may be flat. Also, one noise can help block out another unwanted noise. An example is when loud music in an office drowns out the sounds of typewriters.

Sound is made by air pressure on your eardrums. When you clap your hands, for example, listen to the sound. Air was pushed out from between your hands when you brought them together. At almost the same time, air in your ears pushed your eardrums inward. Your ears signaled your brain to give you the feeling of a clap sound.

The number of sound waves hitting your eardrums each second controls   ●
the highness or lowness of the sound you hear. The strength of sound waves is measured by a sound level meter. The meter uses units called decibels. A whisper amounts to about 20 decibels. A jet plane 100 feet away is about 140 decibels. A sound of about 120 decibels can hurt the ears. Eventually, the ear becomes damaged from such loud noises. People who work in such fields as heavy equipment operation must take care to protect their hearing. It's a good thing that the average speaking voice reaches only 60 decibels. Otherwise, we might all be a little deaf.

Recalling Facts

1. Noise is often called
   - □ a. expected sound.
   - □ b. air pollution.
   - □ c. unwanted sound.

2. Loud noises can cause
   - □ a. death.
   - □ b. a loss of hearing.
   - □ c. poor eyesight.

3. Sound is made by air pressure on your
   - □ a. eardrums.
   - □ b. lungs.
   - □ c. throat.

4. The strength of a whisper is about
   - □ a. 20 decibels.
   - □ b. 40 decibels.
   - □ c. 60 decibels.

5. The sound of a jet plane 100 feet away measures about
   - □ a. 100 decibels.
   - □ b. 120 decibels.
   - □ c. 140 decibels.

Understanding the Passage

6. This article is about
   - □ a. ear pollution.
   - □ b. jet plane noises.
   - □ c. sound level meters.

7. Listening to amplified rock-and-roll music can result in
   - □ a. lack of balance.
   - □ b. slight hearing loss.
   - □ c. weight gain.

8. The writer hints that
   - □ a. noise can cause illness.
   - □ b. many people are born deaf.
   - □ c. sound is always pleasing.

9. We hear when the ear sends a message to the
   - □ a. brain.
   - □ b. eyes.
   - □ c. heart.

10. Noises that are over 120 decibels are
    - □ a. harmful.
    - □ b. helpful.
    - □ c. peaceful.

24   A New Way of Life

The history of our form of government begins with its settlers. Most of the early settlers came from England. They lived in groups called colonies. The King of England was their ruler.

The English settlers founded the Virginia colony at Jamestown in 1607. It was the first permanent English colony. In 1620 other English people came to America. They were known as Pilgrims. They went to Holland first. In Holland, their children began to forget the English ways. They decided to leave Holland and go to the New World. They founded Plymouth colony in Massachusetts. They struggled to build homes and to exist. After a hard winter, the Pilgrims who survived held a feast with the Indians who had helped them begin their new way of life. They thanked God for their blessings. This was the first American Thanksgiving.

More Englishmen, as well as people from other European countries, came to live in America. Many, like the Pilgrims, wanted to be free to worship God in their own way. Others were looking for political freedom. Traders were seeking to make money. The poor and the unemployed people wanted jobs and the chance to earn a better living. Businessmen who had money to invest saw promise of success in America.

After many years, all of the colonists came under British rule. Georgia, founded in 1733, was the last colony to be formed. In 1776, there were thirteen British colonies in the part of America that later became the United States. These colonies became the first thirteen states.

The King let the colonists elect representatives and make local laws. The colonists were free in many ways. But, as time passed, more and more laws for the colonists were made in Great Britain. Under these laws, the colonists had to pay more taxes. However, the colonists were not asked to help make these laws. They had no spokesmen in Great Britain. They began to feel that some of their rights were being taken away from them. They said they could be taxed only by their own officials. The King refused to change the tax laws.

The colonists decided to hold a meeting to discuss their problems. All of the colonies except Georgia sent men to this meeting. It was held in Philadelphia in 1774. It was the First Continental Congress. They asked the King for their rights as Englishmen.

Recalling Facts

1. Most of the early settlers of the United States came from
   - ☐ a. Germany.
   - ☐ b. Denmark.
   - ☐ c. England.

2. Jamestown, Virginia, was founded in the early
   - ☐ a. 1500s.
   - ☐ b. 1600s.
   - ☐ c. 1700s.

3. Before the Pilgrims came to America, they lived in
   - ☐ a. France.
   - ☐ b. Scotland.
   - ☐ c. Holland.

4. The last colony to be founded was
   - ☐ a. Rhode Island.
   - ☐ b. Georgia.
   - ☐ c. Virginia.

5. The Continental Congress was held in
   - ☐ a. Philadelphia.
   - ☐ b. Boston.
   - ☐ c. New York City.

Understanding the Passage

6. Most of the first people who came to America were seeking
   - ☐ a. wealth and opportunity.
   - ☐ b. religious freedom.
   - ☐ c. better jobs.

7. The colonists turned against the King of England when they could not
   - ☐ a. make their own money.
   - ☐ b. send representatives to England.
   - ☐ c. trade with other countries.

8. At the First Continental Congress, the officials did not hear any
   - ☐ a. discussion of rights and freedoms.
   - ☐ b. talk about England.
   - ☐ c. speeches from Georgia delegates.

9. The Pilgrims came to America when
   - ☐ a. their children began to forget their English ways.
   - ☐ b. they heard that the streets in America were paved with gold.
   - ☐ c. the King of England would not allow them to stay in England.

10. We can conclude that
    - ☐ a. people from many different countries lived in the colonies.
    - ☐ b. the King of England was a weak ruler.
    - ☐ c. early colonists wanted to break away from England.

25 A Good Start

A child grows faster during the first few years of life than at any other time. Thus, good nutrition is very important.

Milk is the child's first food. It has a large amount of the nutrients needed during the first two years of life. The kind of milk or formula must be chosen with care.

Human milk is custom-made for the baby. It is clean and pure. It saves a lot of work. Nursing can also be a satisfying experience for both mother and baby. Human milk will usually supply enough of all the important nutrients during the first few months of life, except for vitamin D, fluoride, and iron.

If a prepared formula, evaporated milk, or homogenized milk is used, it will usually have vitamin D added to it. If not, the baby will need to be given vitamin D in addition to its regular milk.

The baby needs vitamin C early in life. Human milk and prepared formulas usually have good amounts of vitamin C. If the baby is being fed evaporated milk or cow's milk formula, the vitamin C should be given in the form of drops. Otherwise a fresh, frozen, or canned fruit juice that is naturally rich in vitamin C can be used.

A source of iron should also be added when the child is one to three months old. Slowly, other foods, such as egg yolk, strained meat, and fish, are added. Be careful when choosing the baby's food. Store-bought strained foods vary widely. They vary in the amount of calories and other nutrients they contain. This is why many mothers decide to prepare their own baby food at home. There they will know what their babies are getting. Your baby will be happier and healthier if you choose foods carefully.

By the time the baby is six months old, he or she will be taking some "table food." When seven to nine months old, a baby is usually ready for foods that are chopped. By then, he or she will likely be eating three meals a day. Still, for a baby's first year of life, formula or mother's milk is the most important food. When a baby is ready to move from milk to other solid foods, it will let you know. The baby might increase the number of bottles it has each day, which lets you know that more filling foods are needed.

Recalling Facts

1. A child's first food is
   - ☐ a. juice.
   - ☐ b. milk.
   - ☐ c. water.

2. Human milk does not supply enough vitamin D, fluoride, and
   - ☐ a. iron.
   - ☐ b. salt.
   - ☐ c. sugar.

3. A prepared formula contains good amounts of
   - ☐ a. fat.
   - ☐ b. starch.
   - ☐ c. vitamin C.

4. A doctor may give a baby iron drops when the child is one or two
   - ☐ a. hours old.
   - ☐ b. days old.
   - ☐ c. months old.

5. A nine-month-old child is ready for foods that are
   - ☐ a. chopped.
   - ☐ b. spicy.
   - ☐ c. fried.

Understanding the Passage

6. Choose the best title for this article.
   - ☐ a. Baby's First Foods
   - ☐ b. The Importance of Iron
   - ☐ c. Learning to Walk

7. What is the main idea of this article?
   - ☐ a. Good nutrition is important for an infant.
   - ☐ b. Many infants eat too much.
   - ☐ c. Vitamin D is the most important vitamin.

8. Vitamin C can be found in most
   - ☐ a. fruit juices.
   - ☐ b. red meats.
   - ☐ c. starchy foods.

9. Strained meat is added to a baby's diet
   - ☐ a. all at once.
   - ☐ b. gradually.
   - ☐ c. not at all.

10. A child starts eating three meals a day when it is about
    - ☐ a. one month old.
    - ☐ b. nine months old.
    - ☐ c. twenty-four months old.

Breads and cereals are healthy and convenient. They are cheap and fit easily into meal plans. Some cost just cents per serving. Even though they are cheap, the whole-grain or enriched products have good amounts of vitamins and minerals. One food study showed that just 20 cents of each food dollar went for flour, cereals, and bakery products.

To help you get your money's worth from breads and cereals, there are some things you should keep in mind. Whole-grain or enriched foods have much more nutrition than unenriched products. Most white bread is enriched. Some special breads, such as French, Italian, and raisin, and many other bake shop products are also enriched. Check the wrapper or ask the baker to be sure.

You should also know that it takes three pounds of unenriched white bread to give the amount of thiamine that is contained in one pound of enriched bread at a much lower price. A pound of whole wheat bread also costs less than three of unenriched white bread, while providing the same nutritional value. Also remember, a large loaf of bread does not always weigh more or contain more food value than a small loaf. Compare prices of equal *weights* of bread to find the better buy. The weight is shown on the wrapper.

Spaghetti, macaroni, and noodles in packages marked "enriched" are more nutritious and usually cost no more than unenriched ones. Enriched rice is more nutritious than white milled rice. It costs more but the extra food value it provides is well worth the cost.

Ready-to-serve cereals in packs of small boxes are expensive. They may cost two or three times as much per ounce as the same cereal in a large box. Pre-sugared cereals cost more per ounce than unsweetened ones. Sugared cereals have more calories but less food value. Cereals you sweeten yourself are a better buy. Cereals you cook yourself almost always cost less than ready-prepared ones.

It may help to know that day-old bread and baked goods may be bought at a great saving. Ask or watch for these in stores where you shop. Baked goods made at home are a good idea. They often cost less than ready-baked products. When made at home with enriched flour, they may have more nutrition, too.

So the next time you shop, make sure you are getting the most nutrition for your money.

Recalling Facts

1. How much out of every food dollar goes for flour, cereals, and bakery products?
   □ a. 20 cents
   □ b. 50 cents
   □ c. 64 cents

2. Unenriched products are not as nutritious as
   □ a. milled foods.
   □ b. packaged foods.
   □ c. whole-grain foods.

3. How many pounds of unenriched bread does it take to give the amount of thiamine in one pound of enriched bread?
   □ a. two
   □ b. three
   □ c. four

4. To get the best bread buy, compare the
   □ a. flavors.
   □ b. weights.
   □ c. prices.

5. To make sure a product is enriched, you should check the
   □ a. price.
   □ b. store.
   □ c. wrapper.

Understanding the Passage

6. What is the main idea of this passage?
   □ a. Breads and cereals provide nutrition and taste.
   □ b. Milled rice is not as nutritious as enriched rice.
   □ c. Ready-baked products are not very expensive.

7. This article hints that
   □ a. breads and cereals are expensive.
   □ b. unenriched foods are high in vitamins.
   □ c. whole-grain foods are nutritious.

8. It's cheaper to buy
   □ a. pre-sweetened cereal.
   □ b. small boxes of cereal.
   □ c. cereals cooked at home.

9. Pre-sugared cereals are
   □ a. just as nutritious as enriched cereals.
   □ b. not very popular with most parents.
   □ c. not as nutritious as unsweetened cereals.

10. When you bake homemade pastry, it's a good idea to use
    □ a. brown sugar.
    □ b. enriched flour.
    □ c. milled rice.

27 Bridging the Gap

Bridges come in a few basic styles. There are beam, arch, cantilever, and suspension bridges. The first two are thousands of years old. The others are not much newer. The bridge is man's oldest building achievement. Even early man built bridges.

Simple beam bridges were not hard to make. Dragging the rocks into place only needed some effort. Today in England, huge slabs of rocks still stand on piers across streams. These simple bridges were also found on long-dry stream beds. They've been there since prehistoric times.

The arch was used in temples and tombs long before it was used for bridges. Roman engineers built stone-arch bridges all over their empire. The most famous stone-arch bridge was Old London Bridge. This was built in 1176. It was made of 19 semicircular stone arches of different lengths. These arches were mounted on thick piers on the Thames River. Soon buildings appeared on the famous bridge. Although loaded with houses and shops, Old London Bridge never fell down. It was always fixed just in time. In the 1820s it was replaced by a new stone-arch bridge. In turn, this was also replaced in the 1960s in order to handle more traffic.

In bridge terms, a cantilever is a diamond-shaped structure. It is balanced on a pier. Two cantilevers, linked by a short support, form a very strong bridge.

We can only guess that man built suspension bridges at an early date. These early bridges were made of tough vines hung over a gorge. Branches were laid across the vines to form a roadway. In China long ago, kites were used to fly the vines across the gorge. Hundreds of such bridges were also built in South America.

Suspension bridges are compared in length of main span. The main span refers to the suspended path between the two towers. The Humber Bridge in Hull, England, is the world's longest suspension bridge. Suspension bridges were once weak structures. They could fall down at any time. They crumpled under the marching feet of soldiers. They fell under droves of cattle. Even heavy loads of snow could make them collapse. They blew down in storms and scared travelers with their swaying. Then, a stronger metal support was added. Suddenly suspension bridges became strong and secure.

Can you imagine traveling over a swaying bridge? It's a good thing the suspension bridge improved.

Recalling Facts

1. Some of the oldest bridges are found in
   - ☐ a. America.
   - ☐ b. Canada.
   - ☐ c. England.

2. The arch was first used in temples and
   - ☐ a. houses.
   - ☐ b. shops.
   - ☐ c. tombs.

3. Early suspension bridges were made of
   - ☐ a. metal.
   - ☐ b. stones.
   - ☐ c. vines.

4. Many suspension bridges were built by people who lived in China and
   - ☐ a. Australia.
   - ☐ b. North America.
   - ☐ c. South America.

5. The longest suspension bridge in the world is the
   - ☐ a. Golden Gate Bridge.
   - ☐ b. Severin Bridge.
   - ☐ c. Humber Bridge.

Understanding the Passage

6. Which of the following is thought to be one of the oldest type bridges?
   - ☐ a. arch
   - ☐ b. cantilever
   - ☐ c. suspension

7. Simple beam bridges were used to cross
   - ☐ a. oceans.
   - ☐ b. gorges.
   - ☐ c. streams.

8. Which type of bridge was popular with the Romans?
   - ☐ a. beam
   - ☐ b. arch
   - ☐ c. suspension

9. Long ago, the Chinese knew how to fly
   - ☐ a. airplanes.
   - ☐ b. balloons.
   - ☐ c. kites.

10. Suspension bridges were once very
    - ☐ a. colorful.
    - ☐ b. dangerous.
    - ☐ c. slippery.

In the age of electricity, most of us have forgotten how to build a simple fire. This is easily remedied.

Safety comes first. Fire is a wonderful ally but a dangerous enemy. When camping, clear a ten-foot circle down to mineral soil or rock. In the home fireplace, there should be a good, strong fire screen to prevent sparks or brands from popping or rolling into the room.

Lay your fire by piling your tinder in a close pile about the size of a hat. Then crisscross the smallest and driest kindling over the tinder. With your back to the wind, light the tinder. The wind will quickly spread the flames ● through the pile. If there is no wind, fan the fire with something. Add the rest of the kindling.

How you add wood now will depend on what the fire is for. If you are cooking, there are a number of styles you can copy from the woodsman. The trapper's fire uses two fairly large logs laid on each side of the fire. It helps to flatten the top of the logs with an ax. Then pots and pans can rest on the logs, and you have a narrow, controlled fire that is easy to fuel ● and easy to cook on.

Some like the lazyman fire, where longer logs come into the fire like spokes from a wheel. The logs are pushed in as they burn and need a larger clearing for safety.

The picturesque hunter's fire has forked sticks supporting a cross pole over the fire from which pothooks can hold the pots and pans at any desired height.

There are many other choices including trench fires to save fuel, rock fireplaces, platform fireplaces, or the reflector fires that are built in front of a tent.

Flames are best for boiling food, but coals are best for broiling. To get ● flames, add a pine knot, kindling or dry twigs. To get coals, you must wait for the wood to burn down to the coals, or you might add charred brands or charcoal from an old fire if available. Allow a full hour from the time the fire is started until the cooking is started.

You can be pretty adventuresome with open-fire cooking. One idea is to use different types of wood to flavor foods. Driftwood, for instance, is excellent for seafood, and apple wood works well with bacon. Enjoy!

Recalling Facts

1. The fire which looks like a wheel with spokes is called the
   - ☐ a. lazyman fire.
   - ☐ b. hunter's fire.
   - ☐ c. trench fire.

2. What is the best fire condition for boiling food?
   - ☐ a. flames
   - ☐ b. coals
   - ☐ c. smoke

3. According to this selection, adding pine knots to a fire creates
   - ☐ a. a fragrance.
   - ☐ b. coals.
   - ☐ c. flames.

4. How much time does a fire need to become suitable for broiling?
   - ☐ a. 15 minutes
   - ☐ b. 30 minutes
   - ☐ c. 60 minutes

5. A fire that supposedly saves fuel is the
   - ☐ a. star fire.
   - ☐ b. hunter's fire.
   - ☐ c. trench fire.

Understanding the Passage

6. The "trapper's fire" is used to
   - ☐ a. cook food.
   - ☐ b. keep warm after dark.
   - ☐ c. lure animals out of the woods.

7. The article suggests that the smallest size of wood is called
   - ☐ a. fuelwood.
   - ☐ b. tinder.
   - ☐ c. kindling.

8. Adding apple wood to a fire
   - ☐ a. puts out the fire.
   - ☐ b. makes the heat more intense.
   - ☐ c. gives food a good taste.

9. In this article, the author warns against
   - ☐ a. carelessness in handling fire.
   - ☐ b. using green wood to start a fire.
   - ☐ c. lighting campfires without permission.

10. The reader may conclude that building a fire is
    - ☐ a. mostly luck.
    - ☐ b. a skill that most people cannot learn.
    - ☐ c. not difficult if you know how.

An owner should start training a dog as soon as possible after getting it. A dog will be eager to please its master. Puppies should be about three months old before any training except housebreaking is started. Many organizations and dog clubs have obedience training.

When training a dog, one must never beat it. A slap on the rump or scolding is enough. In obedience training, simple, one-word commands should be used.

Commands should be given in a firm voice. When a dog obeys a command, the master should praise it in a gentle voice and reward it with a few pats on the head. Each obedience lesson should last no longer than fifteen minutes. The master should give several lessons a day.

The first obedience training should be given at home. Then lessons can be given away from home. After awhile, it will learn to obey anywhere in all kinds of situations.

Most dogs can sleep happily inside the home or out. However, sick dogs, old dogs, and short-haired dogs need special housing.

If a dog is to be kept outside, a doghouse and a pen will be needed. The house should be large enough so the dog can turn around inside. It should be small enough so it can keep it warm with its body heat.

The roof must be built over the door of the house to keep out rain and snow. The roof should be removable so the house can be easily cleaned.

The floor of the house should be off the ground so water will not drain into the bedding. A window or shutter is needed for air to come in.

Old clothing, blankets, or some other warm material would make a good bed for it. The bed must be kept dry and clean.

A pen might be 10 to 15 feet long and about 10 feet wide around the doghouse. The owner should use wire fencing high enough so the dog cannot jump over it, and he or she should bury the bottom edge about 6 inches deep so the dog cannot dig under it.

Many people build a special dog run for their dog. This is simply a cable that is attached to two points at least fifteen feet apart and ten feet above the ground. One end might be a fence, the other side a pole. The dog's leash is attached and it can run freely.

Recalling Facts

1. How old should puppies be before training is begun?
   - ☐ a. six weeks
   - ☐ b. one month
   - ☐ c. three months

2. Obedience training should consist of
   - ☐ a. hand movements.
   - ☐ b. sentence commands.
   - ☐ c. one-word commands.

3. The author advises rewarding a puppy with
   - ☐ a. pats on the head.
   - ☐ b. bones.
   - ☐ c. extra food.

4. Obedience sessions should last no longer than
   - ☐ a. five minutes.
   - ☐ b. fifteen minutes.
   - ☐ c. one hour.

5. The roof on a doghouse should be
   - ☐ a. shingled.
   - ☐ b. insulated.
   - ☐ c. removable.

Understanding the Passage

6. Training should begin when a dog is very young because
   - ☐ a. old dogs cannot learn new tricks.
   - ☐ b. young dogs want to please their owners.
   - ☐ c. puppies are afraid of discipline.

7. The author states that praises and commands should be given
   - ☐ a. after the dog is rewarded.
   - ☐ b. along with hand gestures.
   - ☐ c. in different tones of voice.

8. According to the author, obedience training should begin
   - ☐ a. at home.
   - ☐ b. in unfamiliar surroundings.
   - ☐ c. in stress situations.

9. The author implies that
   - ☐ a. German shepherds are easy to train.
   - ☐ b. dogs should be fed once a day.
   - ☐ c. dogs that are kept in pens sometimes dig their way out.

10. From the information provided, we can assume that
   - ☐ a. housebreaking a dog is the first step in obedience training.
   - ☐ b. dogs should not be allowed to sleep inside a house.
   - ☐ c. some breeds of dogs require vitamins with their meals.

Did you ever stop to think how important water is? All animals and plants are mostly water. A person's body is about 65 percent water. Each of us needs to drink at least five pints of water each day. Big animals need about 15 gallons of water a day.

Water has other uses, too. It is used for washing and air conditioning. It is used for household work and gardening. Steel, gasoline, paper, and most other products are made with the help of water. Power plants use water for cooling. Farms, of course, need water to grow food.

Water is even used to carry goods and people around the world. Water is used for swimming, boating, and other kinds of recreation. Water is the home of many animals and plants, such as fish, whales, clams, and seaweeds.

We can easily see that life would be impossible without water. That is why it is so important to keep our water clean and usable. Yet, polluted water is becoming very common.

Water that has become polluted is unsafe to use. Pollution can happen when sewage and other untreated wastes have been dumped into it. Polluted water can smell, have garbage floating in it, and be unfit for swimming or boating. But even water that looks clean and smells good can be polluted. It may be loaded with germs and dangerous chemicals that you cannot see.

People pollute water in a lot of ways. One way is to allow bathroom and factory wastes to flow through pipes and into waterways without being treated. Another way is to allow soil, fertilizers, and industrial wastes to wash from farms, building sites, and mining sites into waterways after a rain.

Bacteria can feed on some wastes. Other wastes can be diluted by water in waterways. But nature can only do so much. Man is making more waste than nature can handle. More and better wastewater treatment is needed.

It is a fact that not all towns properly treat their drinking water. Many people think that the water they drink is safe. Most of the time it is. But about 4,000 Americans become sick each year from germs in unsafe drinking water. Many more cases are not reported.

Clean water is so important to our lives. We should make an effort to make sure we will have enough of it.

Recalling Facts

1. What percent of a person's body is water?
   - ☐ a. 25 percent
   - ☐ b. 50 percent
   - ☐ c. 65 percent

2. Each of us needs at least five pints of water a
   - ☐ a. day.
   - ☐ b. week.
   - ☐ c. month.

3. Water is used to make
   - ☐ a. coal.
   - ☐ b. gold.
   - ☐ c. steel.

4. Power plants use water for
   - ☐ a. boating.
   - ☐ b. cooling.
   - ☐ c. transportation.

5. About how many cases of illness caused by drinking unsafe water are reported each year in America?
   - ☐ a. 2,000
   - ☐ b. 4,000
   - ☐ c. 10,000

Understanding the Passage

6. This article suggests that polluted water
   - ☐ a. always looks dirty.
   - ☐ b. carries many germs.
   - ☐ c. is not very common.

7. This article is mostly about
   - ☐ a. freshwater animals.
   - ☐ b. the importance of water.
   - ☐ c. popular waterways.

8. Polluted water
   - ☐ a. always has an odor.
   - ☐ b. is usually found near the ocean.
   - ☐ c. sometimes looks safe and clean.

9. Water often becomes polluted because we allow
   - ☐ a. oil barges to travel the waterways.
   - ☐ b. people to swim and boat in clean water.
   - ☐ c. untreated wastes to enter our waterways.

10. Which of the following can help keep our water clean?
    - ☐ a. stronger chemicals
    - ☐ b. treatment plants
    - ☐ c. wire fences

31 The Needs of the People

The United States Constitution has been changed to serve the needs of the people. When it was accepted in 1789, there were no large cities. There were no railroads and very few factories. Most of the people lived on farms. Today, most people live in cities. Their lives are tied together. Our government had to serve new needs of the nation as they arose. How was this done?

The Constitution has developed through general laws. The Congress, the President, and the courts have needed help to carry out their duties. Boards have been set up to study the needs of the people and to advise the Congress of changes that should be made in the laws. The Congress has set up other government boards and offices with authority to make rules.

The Congress has passed laws giving the President more departments in the Cabinet. In 1789, there were only four departments. Today there are eleven departments. The Congress has added new federal courts as they have been needed. By these and other general laws, the Congress has helped to organize the government under the Constitution. The government has been changed to meet the new needs of the people.

The Constitution has developed also through treaties. The United States must get along well with other nations. We trade with people in many lands. The ships of other nations often carry our goods. Our citizens travel, live, and die in other countries. The citizens of other nations live and trade here.

The writers of the Constitution did not know what matters should be covered by treaties. They decided to let the President and the Senate develop this part of the Constitution. They declared in Article II that the President "shall have power, by and with the advice and consent of the Senate, to make treaties, provided two-thirds of the senators present concur."

The Constitution does not say when or on what subjects treaties shall be made. These matters are left to the President and to the Senate. For example, the Constitution does not say whether citizens of other countries can own land in the United States. But the President and the Senate have made treaties with other nations giving their citizens the right to own land in the United States. Texas came into the Union by a treaty with the United States. These are two examples that show how treaties help to give life to the Constitution.

Recalling Facts

1. The Constitution was
   accepted in
   ☐ a. 1776.
   ☐ b. 1789.
   ☐ c. 1823.

2. The greatest number of people
   today live in
   ☐ a. cities.
   ☐ b. towns.
   ☐ c. rural areas.

3. How many departments
   did the first United States
   Cabinet have?
   ☐ a. three
   ☐ b. four
   ☐ c. five

4. What state came into the
   Union by a treaty?
   ☐ a. Arizona
   ☐ b. Texas
   ☐ c. Georgia

5. To help carry out its duties,
   the Congress sets up
   ☐ a. departments.
   ☐ b. boards.
   ☐ c. courts.

Understanding the Passage

6. According to the article, the
   ☐ a. Constitution has
        been rewritten.
   ☐ b. government has
        been changed.
   ☐ c. role of the President
        has been changed.

7. The Constitution is able to
   meet the changing needs of the
   country through
   ☐ a. treaties.
   ☐ b. declarations.
   ☐ c. popular votes.

8. The author uses "treaty" to mean
   ☐ a. law.
   ☐ b. agreement.
   ☐ c. power.

9. Article II of the Constitution
   deals with
   ☐ a. Presidential power.
   ☐ b. foreign countries.
   ☐ c. trade agreements.

10. The author states that Congress
    ☐ a. makes laws.
    ☐ b. enforces laws.
    ☐ c. breaks laws.

32   A Major Concern

There is good reason to be concerned with the eating habits of teenagers. During the teen years, good food habits may be lost. The teenage appetite is often big. But a large appetite isn't always that important. Even with a big appetite, teenagers may not get the good foods they need. Teenage boys and girls grow at a fast rate. Except for infancy, the growth is faster than at any other time. A boy has great nutritional needs during the teen years. His needs are greater than at any other time in his life. The needs of a girl becoming a woman are great. Only during pregnancy and the period following the birth are they greater.

A teenage boy may suddenly shoot up as much as four inches in height. He may gain fifteen pounds a year. A teenage girl's total gain is not quite as large, but it is considerable. Growth means more than adding inches and weight. It means that body fat is lost while bones increase in density. Muscles develop in size and strength.

Teenage eating habits are often poor. The reasons are not hard to find. School, clubs, and part-time jobs keep teenagers away from home at mealtimes. Their eating habits are influenced more by friends than by parents. Some skip breakfast because they don't have enough time for it. Some choose snacks that are too rich in fats and sugar. Teenage girls sometimes eat too little because they do not want to get fat. Diets have to be well planned for both boys and girls. Each has a great need for protein and vitamins. The need is so great that they cannot afford to fill up on foods that have empty calories. Most of the time a teenage boy winds up with a better diet than a girl. This happens simply because the boy has a bigger appetite and eats more. But some boys may shy away from foods that have important nutrients. Instead, they may eat great amounts of junk food. Sometimes this creates a weight problem.

The overweight teenager may eat the same kinds of food as his average friend, but too much of them. Rich desserts and snack foods should be replaced with fresh fruits and vegetables.

Instead of a crash diet to take off pounds, overweight teenagers should develop the well-balanced eating habits that they need for the rest of their lives.

Recalling Facts

1. The teenager has a big
   - ☐ a. appetite.
   - ☐ b. stomach.
   - ☐ c. voice.

2. The growth rate during the teen years is not as rapid as it is during
   - ☐ a. infancy.
   - ☐ b. puberty.
   - ☐ c. adolescence.

3. In a year, a teenage boy may gain as much as
   - ☐ a. two pounds.
   - ☐ b. five pounds.
   - ☐ c. fifteen pounds.

4. Who has the most influence on teenage eating habits?
   - ☐ a. doctors
   - ☐ b. friends
   - ☐ c. parents

5. Some teenagers choose snacks that are too rich in fats and
   - ☐ a. minerals.
   - ☐ b. protein.
   - ☐ c. sugar.

Understanding the Passage

6. During the teen years, good food habits often
   - ☐ a. develop.
   - ☐ b. disappear.
   - ☐ c. remain.

7. This article hints that teenagers
   - ☐ a. choose good foods.
   - ☐ b. grow very quickly.
   - ☐ c. like loud sounds.

8. We can see that during the teen years
   - ☐ a. bones and muscles get stronger.
   - ☐ b. growing bones break easily.
   - ☐ c. many boys and girls become ill.

9. Teenagers seem to be very
   - ☐ a. active.
   - ☐ b. lazy.
   - ☐ c. sad.

10. Teenage girls do not want to
    - ☐ a. get a job.
    - ☐ b. grow taller.
    - ☐ c. gain weight.

Fibers have been used for making cloth for thousands of years. Many of them are still used today to make fabric. Linen, for example, is the oldest textile fabric. It comes from the flax plant. It was used in prehistoric times and in ancient Egypt. We have learned that linen was woven in England as early as the year 400. Today this fiber is used in many ways around the home. In fact, the word "linens" has come to be used as the name for household textile goods, such as sheets and towels.

Wool also dates back as far as Bible times. Much later, in the 15th and 16th centuries, sheep from Spain and England were brought to the American colonies. Spanish explorers brought sheep with them to California and Florida. Thus, wool came to be used here in America.

Another leading fiber is cotton. It was woven into fabrics in India as early as 1500 years before Christ. Cotton was also used for candlewicks in England as far back as the 1300s. By the 1400s, cotton fabrics were being manufactured in central Europe. In 1793 in the southern United States, Eli Whitney invented the "cotton engine." This name was later shortened to become the "cotton gin." It was used to comb seeds out of cotton fibers. This machine removed a major delay in the processing of cotton. Because of it, cotton became the South's most important crop.

The production of silk began with the ancient Chinese. Legend says that a Chinese empress saw a silkworm spinning its cocoon. The empress wondered how she would look in a gown made of such fine material. Silk weaving soon spread. It was seen in many other countries. But silkworm raising remained wholly Chinese until the sixth century. At that time, the art spread to other parts of the Middle East.

The fibers that have been mentioned so far are all natural. But today there are many man-made fibers in use. Some of these were made for a certain need. Others were discovered mostly by chance. Production of man-made fiber was chiefly a United States industry until the 1950s. After the 1950s things changed. Foreign production grew until, by 1960, this country made less than half of the world's man-made fibers. Rayon and nylon are just a few examples of today's man-made fabrics.

*Reading Time*_____ *Comprehension Score*_____ *Words per Minute*_____   79

Recalling Facts

1. The oldest textile fabric is
   - ☐ a. cotton.
   - ☐ b. linen.
   - ☐ c. silk.

2. Wool was brought to California and Florida by the
   - ☐ a. American Indians.
   - ☐ b. French traders.
   - ☐ c. Spanish explorers.

3. Cotton was woven into fabrics in India as early as
   - ☐ a. Columbus's first voyage.
   - ☐ b. the late 1300s.
   - ☐ c. 1500 years before Christ.

4. Silk production began with the
   - ☐ a. ancient Chinese.
   - ☐ b. early Spanish colonists.
   - ☐ c. first English explorers.

5. Which of the following is a man-made fiber?
   - ☐ a. cotton
   - ☐ b. linen
   - ☐ c. rayon

Understanding the Passage

6. Which of the following is most likely true?
   - ☐ a. American colonists did not know how to weave.
   - ☐ b. Linen is an extremely old fabric.
   - ☐ c. The Spanish were the first to use silk.

7. Wool comes from
   - ☐ a. an animal.
   - ☐ b. a mineral.
   - ☐ c. a plant.

8. This article hints that
   - ☐ a. cotton was used in India before it was used in America.
   - ☐ b. the southern United States once raised many sheep.
   - ☐ c. no one knows how the flax plant came to America.

9. Silk comes from a
   - ☐ a. type of insect.
   - ☐ b. green, leafy plant.
   - ☐ c. vitamin.

10. We can see from this article that fabrics
    - ☐ a. are costly to make and ship.
    - ☐ b. can be natural or man-made.
    - ☐ c. change with the fashion.

Every year a great number of babies and young children die or are injured in fires. One out of every five fires is caused by careless smoking or by children playing with matches and lighters. Don't tempt children by leaving matches or lighters around a room.

Never leave a child alone in a house. In just a few seconds they could start a fire. Or a fire could start and trap them. A child will panic in a fire and will not know what to do. Unless a parent is around to help, a child may try to hide under a bed or in a closet. Home fire drills are a sound idea. The best way to stop panic in case of fire is to know what to do before a fire breaks out.

Your first thought in a fire should always be escape. Far too many people become victims because they do not know the killing power and speed of fire. If a fire is very small and has just started, you can put it out yourself. Do this if you have the proper tools on hand. In any case always send the children outside first. Smoke, not fire, is the real killer in a blaze. According to studies, as many as eight out of ten deaths in fires are due to inhaling fumes long before the flames ever came near the person.

Burns are another hazard to tots. Fireplaces, space heaters, floor furnaces, and radiators have all caused horrible burns to babies. Since you cannot watch your child all the time, you must screen fireplaces. Put guards around heaters and radiators.

Some people use a vaporizer or portable heater in a child's room. If you do, be sure you place it out of reach. Be sure, too, that it is not placed too close to blankets or bedclothes.

Use care in the kitchen. It is not safe to let an infant crawl or a small child walk around the kitchen while you are preparing meals. There is danger of your tripping and spilling something hot on the child. There is even danger of a child pulling a hot pot off the stove on to herself. Also, do not use tablecloths that hang over the table edge. Children can easily pull the cloth and whatever is on the table down. Be aware of these dangers and protect your child.

Recalling Facts

1. Careless smoking or children playing with matches and lighters cause
   - ☐ a. one out of five fires.
   - ☐ b. two out of three fires.
   - ☐ c. five out of ten fires.

2. Your first thought in a fire should always be
   - ☐ a. panic.
   - ☐ b. prevention.
   - ☐ c. escape.

3. What is the real killer in a fire?
   - ☐ a. flames
   - ☐ b. fuel
   - ☐ c. smoke

4. How many people die in fires from inhaling deadly smoke fumes?
   - ☐ a. two out of three
   - ☐ b. five out of eight
   - ☐ c. eight out of ten

5. Burns can be caused by
   - ☐ a. harmful toys.
   - ☐ b. old tin cans.
   - ☐ c. space heaters.

Understanding the Passage

6. We can see that
   - ☐ a. adults know how to handle fires.
   - ☐ b. many children start fires in the home.
   - ☐ c. some firefighters are not well trained.

7. When children are trapped in a fire, they often become
   - ☐ a. confused.
   - ☐ b. happy.
   - ☐ c. silly.

8. The best way to stop panic in the case of fire is to
   - ☐ a. be prepared.
   - ☐ b. call a neighbor.
   - ☐ c. run away.

9. Using vaporizers in a child's room can be
   - ☐ a. dangerous.
   - ☐ b. funny.
   - ☐ c. untidy.

10. Many fires start because
    - ☐ a. fire departments are rare.
    - ☐ b. people don't respect fire.
    - ☐ c. someone was careless.

35 Choosing and Training a Dog

Any of the different types of dogs can be kept as pets. Breeding, size, and other features, however, make some more suitable than others.

The breeds of dogs are divided into six groups. These groups are sporting dogs, hounds, terriers, working dogs, toy dogs, and non-sporting dogs.

In each of these groups the dogs are bred for a special purpose. Many dogs serve the purpose for which they were bred. But many others have become favorite household pets. Some dogs have cropped ears and tails for purposes of style or to meet dog show requirements.

If you buy a purebred dog, you can select one that has traits best suited to your needs. You must be sure to get the certificate that gives the date of birth and the registration number.

It is not necessary to buy a purebred dog to have a good pet. Many "mutts" make excellent pets. Often you can get a mixed-breed dog free or for a small fee from a dog pound, animal shelter, or pet shop.

No matter what its ancestry is, the dog will require some basic training, and housebreaking comes first.

A dog should be trained to relieve itself outdoors on its owner's property so it will not annoy neighbors. In an apartment, a dog owner may need to teach a pet to use newspapers first and then to go outdoors after it has learned to control itself.

If an owner must housebreak a dog on newspapers, several layers should be spread in a little-used part of the home. After the dog has learned to use newspapers, they should be taken away except at night. In the daytime the dog can be taken outdoors when it must go. As it grows older, it will learn to control itself. Then the newspapers can be removed.

When it has an accident, it must be scolded. Then it should be taken to its spot outdoors. The floor must be scrubbed enough to remove even the slightest odor.

When a dog shows signs of restlessness, such as turning and sniffing, it should be taken outside. It must be left outside long enough for it to relieve itself. Then it can be brought in immediately. When the weather is bad, it may not want to go outside. But if it is taken out anyway, it will finish quickly and come back inside.

Recalling Facts

1. Dogs with cropped ears are seen most often in
   - ☐ a. dog shows.
   - ☐ b. hunting areas.
   - ☐ c. sled races.

2. Most purebred dogs are sold with
   - ☐ a. birth certificates.
   - ☐ b. a written guarantee.
   - ☐ c. a license.

3. When a dog has an accident, it should be
   - ☐ a. ignored.
   - ☐ b. scolded.
   - ☐ c. slapped.

4. The first thing a dog needs is
   - ☐ a. cropped ears.
   - ☐ b. basic training.
   - ☐ c. a new leash.

5. The author suggests housebreaking a dog by using
   - ☐ a. a litter box.
   - ☐ b. an old blanket.
   - ☐ c. newspapers.

Understanding the Passage

6. This article is mostly about
   - ☐ a. teaching a dog tricks.
   - ☐ b. buying and training a young dog.
   - ☐ c. taking care of a dog that is ill.

7. A "mutt" is a
   - ☐ a. dog from mixed breeds.
   - ☐ b. person who trains animals.
   - ☐ c. dog that bites.

8. When a dog begins turning and sniffing, it is
   - ☐ a. suffering from a high fever.
   - ☐ b. showing that it is hungry.
   - ☐ c. indicating that it wants to go out.

9. The author implies that
   - ☐ a. a mixed-breed dog does not usually live long.
   - ☐ b. dogs often eat too much food.
   - ☐ c. a hound is not considered to be a sporting dog.

10. The reader can infer that
   - ☐ a. most purebred dogs cost more than $100.
   - ☐ b. mixed-breed dogs are less expensive than purebreds.
   - ☐ c. purebreds are more popular than mixed breeds.

36

Think Before You Throw

Packaging wastes have increased in the past few years. Chances are that they will go right on increasing. One reason for this is that there are more people. Also, each of us is using more packaging materials than ever before.

Take cheese for example. Years ago, the cheese you bought was cut to order from a big wheel. Now it comes wrapped in neat little packages. Another example is the drugstore. In drugstores we serve ourselves from racks of packaged goods. In the past, clerks sold goods from large containers. Today, we rely on the package, not the sales clerk, to sell the product. All these packages add to our solid waste problem.

What can we do to help? One thing is to put as little as possible into the garbage can. Almost nothing is saved and reused once it has been thrown away. It costs too much money to collect and separate wastes. It is cheaper to use new products. It's true that millions of tons of waste are saved and reused each year, but these do not come from the home. Clean waste materials that can be reused come mostly from factories where such materials can be collected, stored, and picked up easily. For instance, cardboard cartons are one item that is now saved in large amounts. This is because the cartons can be easily picked up at retail stores.

Another thing we can do is not to buy more packaged goods than we need. It costs more and it makes more solid wastes. Potato chips are cheaper in the bag. Don't pay extra for a box or can if you don't need the stronger package. Check unit prices for the best buy. For instance, cheese spreads come many ways. If you buy your cheese spread in an aerosol can, you're buying mostly can. You're buying mostly convenience. Be sure that it's worth the price to you. And if your choice means more solid wastes, you should be willing to pay the price of proper disposal. Think of solid wastes before you buy.

More than two-thirds of litter consists of old packages. If you dispose of your wastes in the right places, you are helping to solve the litter problem. Did you know that it costs about 25 cents to pick up and dispose of each item of roadside litter? That's a lot of money and that money is coming out of your tax dollars.

Recalling Facts

1. Years ago cheese was cut from a
   - ☐ a. big wheel.
   - ☐ b. large link.
   - ☐ c. small square.

2. Packaging wastes add to our
   - ☐ a. air pollution.
   - ☐ b. health problems.
   - ☐ c. solid waste problems.

3. Clean waste materials that can be reused come mostly from
   - ☐ a. factories.
   - ☐ b. hospitals.
   - ☐ c. schools.

4. Potato chips are cheaper if they are packed in a
   - ☐ a. bag.
   - ☐ b. box.
   - ☐ c. can.

5. More than two-thirds of litter consists of old
   - ☐ a. cars.
   - ☐ b. clothes.
   - ☐ c. packages.

Understanding the Passage

6. What is this article mostly about?
   - ☐ a. noise pollution
   - ☐ b. solid waste pollution
   - ☐ c. water pollution

7. What is the main idea of this article?
   - ☐ a. Packaging wastes are increasing.
   - ☐ b. Pollution is not always harmful.
   - ☐ c. Stores sell many large cartons.

8. We can see that cardboard cartons are easy to
   - ☐ a. burn.
   - ☐ b. store.
   - ☐ c. reuse.

9. Potato chips that are packed in a can are
   - ☐ a. hard to find.
   - ☐ b. not very fresh.
   - ☐ c. well protected.

10. Getting rid of litter is
   - ☐ a. cheap.
   - ☐ b. easy.
   - ☐ c. expensive.

37

The First Thirteen

The first colonists came to America in 1607. Most were leaving England, but it was still their mother country. The King of England was still their ruler.

Each colony was settled by colonists who came for a purpose. The purpose was not the same in all of the colonies. The colonists in Virginia came to trade. They cut lumber and grew tobacco for sale. The Pilgrims and Puritans, who settled in what is now Massachusetts, came to worship as they pleased. The Quakers came to Pennsylvania and the Roman Catholics came to Maryland for the same purpose.

The Dutch came to trade. They settled in New York. The French colonists settled in Canada and the Spanish colonists settled in Florida. They wanted to trade with the Indians and to teach them the ways of the white man.

One by one the colonies of other nations came under the control of Great Britain. In 1776 there were thirteen British colonies in that part of America that became the United States. These thirteen colonies later became the first thirteen states.

The British people had a king, but they elected representatives who helped make the laws. The lawmaking body was called the Parliament. The people could always tell the lawmakers if they did not like the laws. Sometimes the people were able to have the laws changed.

The king and the Parliament governed the colonies in America. The king let some colonies elect representatives who made some of the local laws. But he sent governors to most of the colonies to carry out the laws of Great Britain. They collected the king's taxes on goods that the colonists brought in from other countries. The colonists were free in many ways. For more than a hundred years they did not say very much against the king and the Parliament.

In 1754 there was a change. A war began between the British colonists and the French. But it was not until 1756 that Great Britain and France actually declared war. In America, the French and British colonists, each with their Indian allies, helped their mother countries. The war was called the French and Indian War.

The British soldiers and the colonists put up a good fight. Great Britain won the war. A peace treaty was signed in 1763 and Great Britain received Canada. The French colonists in Canada then became subjects of Great Britain.

Recalling Facts

1. The colonists who came to Virginia grew
   - ☐ a. corn.
   - ☐ b. wheat.
   - ☐ c. tobacco.

2. The Quakers settled in the area now known as
   - ☐ a. Ohio.
   - ☐ b. Delaware.
   - ☐ c. Pennsylvania.

3. The Dutch came to America to
   - ☐ a. worship.
   - ☐ b. trade.
   - ☐ c. govern themselves.

4. Florida was the site of the first
   - ☐ a. French settlements.
   - ☐ b. Spanish settlements.
   - ☐ c. English settlements.

5. Great Britain and France declared war on each other in the middle
   - ☐ a. 1750s.
   - ☐ b. 1770s.
   - ☐ c. 1790s.

Understanding the Passage

6. During the French and Indian War, colonists
   - ☐ a. sided with their mother countries.
   - ☐ b. supported England.
   - ☐ c. helped the French.

7. As a result of the French and Indian War,
   - ☐ a. the colonists were taxed heavily on foreign goods.
   - ☐ b. many people left France to settle in America.
   - ☐ c. Canada came under English rule.

8. When the settlers first came to America, they
   - ☐ a. set up their own government.
   - ☐ b. gave up the customs of their homelands.
   - ☐ c. remained under British rule.

9. Parliament is described as
   - ☐ a. a lawmaking body of people.
   - ☐ b. the first colonial government.
   - ☐ c. an early American court of law.

10. The author implies that the Indians were
    - ☐ a. savage and cruel.
    - ☐ b. strange and timid.
    - ☐ c. friendly and helpful.

38 **The Right Choice**

Fresh or frozen, canned or dried, instant or from scratch? Which foods have the nutrients? Which do not? The fact is they all do. All foods have their place. And almost all food in its place is good food. Some foods are safer to use when they are processed. Some are more appealing when they are fresh. It's a good idea to know your foods. Packaged, pasteurized, fortified milk has been around for so long that no one thinks of it any more as a processed food, but it is. Because milk is pasteurized, or processed, it is now safe to drink. Unpasteurized milk may carry many germs that can ● make us sick.

Buy cake and cookie mixes, or start from scratch? It depends on how much free time you have. While a cake from a mix can have the same nutritional value as your own, it may also have unwanted chemical preservatives.

Which bread is the best? Whole grain breads and cereals retain the germ and outer layers of grain where the B vitamins are. When wheat is milled into white flour, however, it loses these precious vitamins. Therefore, when you buy white bread, it is wise to choose the enriched kind because of ● added nutrients.

Fresh or frozen? Foods in the frozen food case offer as much food value as those in the produce section of the store. The choice you make depends on which foods you prefer and the amount of money you want to spend. Any loss of vitamin C in frozen fruits is minimal. Well-packaged frozen meat, poultry, and fish are nutritious. They have the same food value as those that are bought right from the butcher or the fish store.

Surprisingly, fresh or raw foods are not always better than canned or frozen ones. It depends on how much they are handled. For instance, leafy, ● dark green vegetables packed in crushed ice keep a lot of their vitamin C on the way to the store. But if they are left to sit for five days or so, they lose about half of it. Cooking will also cause some vitamin loss. Although the loss may be great, these vegetables contain large amounts of vitamins. They still provide good amounts of vitamin C and vitamin A when they are eaten.

Choosing the proper food is no game. It is a serious matter and one that we should pay attention to.

*Reading Time*_____ *Comprehension Score*_____ *Words per Minute*_____ 89

Recalling Facts

1. Unpasteurized milk may carry many
   - ☐ a. chemicals.
   - ☐ b. germs.
   - ☐ c. vitamins.

2. Enriched bread has added
   - ☐ a. color.
   - ☐ b. flavor.
   - ☐ c. nutrients.

3. Frozen fruits lose only a small amount of
   - ☐ a. vitamin A.
   - ☐ b. vitamin B.
   - ☐ c. vitamin C.

4. Frozen meat is nutritious as long as it is properly
   - ☐ a. aged.
   - ☐ b. packaged.
   - ☐ c. stored.

5. Fresh vegetables lose some of their vitamins when they are
   - ☐ a. cooked.
   - ☐ b. packed.
   - ☐ c. pickled.

Understanding the Passage

6. What is this article mostly about?
   - ☐ a. good food
   - ☐ b. junk food
   - ☐ c. poisoned food

7. Processing a food may make it
   - ☐ a. less expensive.
   - ☐ b. more filling.
   - ☐ c. safer to eat.

8. Milk is
   - ☐ a. a long-lasting food.
   - ☐ b. a processed food.
   - ☐ c. an unpackaged food.

9. Whole grain breads are more nutritious than
   - ☐ a. frozen fish and meat.
   - ☐ b. store-bought mixes.
   - ☐ c. white milled wheat.

10. We can see that fresh and frozen foods have
    - ☐ a. many kinds of germs.
    - ☐ b. little vitamin C.
    - ☐ c. the same food value.

Many kinds of insulation can be used for the home. Kinds that are easily installed make good do-it-yourself tasks. These kinds include batts, blankets, and loose fill. Avoid plastic foam. It is best installed by a contractor who has special tools for the job.

Batts and blankets are made of glass fiber or rock wool. Batts come in packs of four-foot lengths or eight-foot lengths. Blankets come in rolls. Both are sold in widths of 15 or 23 inches to fit normal spaces in house frames. Both come in thicknesses of 1 to 7 inches. Both batts and blankets are sold with or without vapor barriers.

To insulate an attic floor, lay batts or blankets between the joists. Batts and blankets can be bought with a vapor barrier on one side. To install, place the barrier face down so that, when it is in place, you no longer see it.

To insulate the floor above a basement, push batts or blankets between the floor joists from below. Be sure that the vapor barrier is facing up, toward the house. To support the insulation, lace wire back and forth between nails spaced two feet apart. Or you may tack chicken wire to the joists.

Instead of batts or blankets, you may insulate with loose fill. It is made from glass fiber, rock wool, cellulose, perlite, or vermiculite. Loose fill tends to settle after a while. Yet, cellulose, which is made from recycled newspaper, makes an excellent insulator. It must, however, be treated to become fire resistant. Use the loose fill to fill in the spaces between the joists. You will have to put in your own vapor barrier. A plastic sheet may be stapled or tacked down before the loose fill is poured.

Your home may already have some insulation. Even so, you may wish to add some more. In that case here are a few hints. Do not put insulation on top of lighting fixtures for the floor below. Keep insulation at least three inches away from such fixtures. Do not cover eave vents with insulation. Be sure that there is enough space in the attic to let moisture out.

A well-insulated home saves you money. It keeps your home cooler in the summer. It also keeps the house warmer in the winter. Don't be afraid to insulate your home yourself. It's really not a difficult job!

Recalling Facts

1. Which of the following insulations is best installed by a contractor?
   - ☐ a. glass fiber
   - ☐ b. plastic foam
   - ☐ c. rock wool

2. Batts and blankets come in thicknesses of
   - ☐ a. 1 to 7 inches.
   - ☐ b. 10 to 12 inches.
   - ☐ c. 15 to 23 inches.

3. Cellulose is made from recycled
   - ☐ a. cloth.
   - ☐ b. plastic.
   - ☐ c. newspaper.

4. Which of the following is a loose fill insulation?
   - ☐ a. batts
   - ☐ b. blankets
   - ☐ c. perlite

5. Loose fill should be used to fill the spaces between the
   - ☐ a. joists.
   - ☐ b. shingles.
   - ☐ c. windows.

Understanding the Passage

6. Many kinds of insulation are
   - ☐ a. easy to install.
   - ☐ b. expensive to buy.
   - ☐ c. harmful to people.

7. The normal spaces in house frames range from
   - ☐ a. 1 to 7 inches.
   - ☐ b. 8 to 10 inches.
   - ☐ c. 15 to 23 inches.

8. If cellulose is not treated, it will
   - ☐ a. burn easily.
   - ☐ b. dry up.
   - ☐ c. hold water.

9. We can see that loose fill does not come with
   - ☐ a. instructions.
   - ☐ b. insulation.
   - ☐ c. a vapor barrier.

10. A well-insulated house saves you money on your
    - ☐ a. food bill.
    - ☐ b. heating bill.
    - ☐ c. water bill.

Domestic cats are classified as either long haired or short haired. Long-haired types were developed in Persia and Afghanistan. Short-haired types were developed in Egypt, Europe, and Asia.

Usually, short-haired cats are active and playful, and easier to care for than long-haired ones. Long-haired cats are quiet, stay-at-home pets, but they sometimes need extra care because of their long hair.

You can buy a bed for your cat or you can make one from a box or basket. The bed should be in a quiet part of the home away from drafts. It should be lined with a blanket, cushion, or discarded clothing. The bedding must be kept clean.

A cat should have a balanced diet. Cat foods from the market usually provide good nourishment under normal conditions.

A cat should not be given small bones that are likely to splinter, especially bones from pork or poultry.

Although a cat may lick its bowl clean, it should be rinsed after each use. Fresh water should be available at all times. The same bowl should not be used for water as is used for food.

Kittens usually are weaned when they are about six to eight weeks old. They keep some of their baby teeth until they reach six months. They must be fed four times a day until they lose their baby teeth.

As the kittens grow, they will gradually eat more food. The number of feedings will decrease to twice daily by the time they are eight or nine months old.

Normally cats should not be bathed. They clean their fur by licking it. If a cat gets dirty, it may be bathed in warm, soapy water.

Its skin must be rubbed thoroughly with a cloth. The water must be kept out of its eyes and ears. It must be rinsed in warm water and dried thoroughly. It must be kept indoors until completely dry.

Cleaning preparations for cats also may be used.

A cat must be brushed often, especially if it has long hair. Brushing gets loose hairs out of its coat that otherwise would get on the furniture and rugs. Knots form in the coats of long-haired cats. The knots can be pulled apart with a comb. If that fails, blunt scissors can be used. Keeping your cat and its eating area clean helps keep away fleas and pests.

Reading Time _____   *Comprehension Score* _____   *Words per Minute* _____

Recalling Facts

1. Long-haired cats were developed in
   □ a. Egypt.
   □ b. Asia.
   □ c. Persia.

2. Long-haired cats tend to be
   □ a. quiet.
   □ b. active.
   □ c. playful.

3. A cat should not be given
   □ a. chicken bones.
   □ b. beef bones.
   □ c. lamb bones.

4. Until kittens lose their baby teeth, they must be fed
   □ a. twice a day.
   □ b. three times a day.
   □ c. four times a day.

5. Kittens are usually weaned when they are no older than
   □ a. four weeks.
   □ b. eight weeks.
   □ c. twelve weeks.

Understanding the Passage

6. The author implies that kittens must be fed often because they
   □ a. like to eat.
   □ b. have small stomachs.
   □ c. digest food slowly.

7. The author recommends
   □ a. bathing cats at least once a month.
   □ b. using scissors for knots in fur.
   □ c. giving cats vitamins.

8. From the facts provided, the reader can assume that
   □ a. water is harmful to a cat's ears.
   □ b. cats enjoy sleeping in paper bags.
   □ c. domestic cats are related to tigers and lions.

9. Cat food that can be purchased in the market
   □ a. is often lacking in important vitamins.
   □ b. contains adequate nutrition for most cats.
   □ c. should not be offered at every meal.

10. We can conclude from the article that cats
    □ a. are fussy eaters.
    □ b. are easy to train.
    □ c. require a minimum of care.

41   An Unexpected Drama

President Lincoln was leaning slightly forward with his hand on the railing. He had turned his head to look into the audience. Pulling back the flag that decorated the box, he was looking between the pillar and the flag. It was at this moment, 10:15 P.M., that John Wilkes Booth entered the door to box 8 and fired the fatal shot. A single-shot derringer, about six inches long, was fired by Booth at close range. The bullet entered Lincoln's head and lodged close behind the right eye. The President slumped forward in his chair and then backward, never to regain consciousness.

Quickly Major Rathbone sprang upon the assassin. Booth dropped the gun, broke from Rathbone's grasp and lunged at him with a large knife. Rathbone received a deep wound in his left arm above the elbow. Booth placed one hand on the railing to the left of the center pillar and jumped over the railing. Rathbone again seized Booth but caught only his clothing. As he leaped, Booth's right boot struck the framed picture of George Washington. The spur on his right heel caught in the fringe of the flag and brought it down, tearing a strip with it. These obstacles caused the assassin to lose his balance, and he fell awkwardly on the stage. He landed in a kneeling position, with his left leg resting on the stage. In the fall, the large bone of his left leg was fractured about two inches above the ankle.

The actor regained his balance like an athlete and is supposed to have waved his dagger and shouted, "Sic Semper Tyrannis" (Thus always with tyrants), before dashing across the stage. Harry Hawk, seeing Booth coming toward him with a knife, ran through the center doorway on the stage and up a flight of stairs.

Leaving the stage on the north side of the theater, Booth passed between Laura Keene and young William J. Ferguson, standing near a desk. In the narrow aisle leading from the stage to the rear door, Booth bumped into William Withers, Jr., the orchestra leader. He slashed twice at Withers, cutting his coat and knocking him to the floor before rushing out the door. Grasping the horse's reins from Mr. Burroughs, Booth felled him with the butt end of his knife. He then mounted the horse and rode swiftly from the alley. History had been made.

Recalling Facts

1. Lincoln was shot while he
   was sitting in
   - ☐ a. the balcony.
   - ☐ b. a box seat.
   - ☐ c. the front row.

2. Lincoln was shot in the
   - ☐ a. morning.
   - ☐ b. afternoon.
   - ☐ c. evening.

3. The person who first tried to
   stop Booth was
   - ☐ a. Ferguson.
   - ☐ b. Withers.
   - ☐ c. Rathbone.

4. Booth injured the greatest
   number of people with his
   - ☐ a. gun.
   - ☐ b. knife.
   - ☐ c. cane.

5. In a fall to the stage, Booth
   fractured his
   - ☐ a. arm.
   - ☐ b. ankle.
   - ☐ c. leg.

Understanding the Passage

6. The author arranges details
   in order of
   - ☐ a. importance.
   - ☐ b. time.
   - ☐ c. interest.

7. This article is mostly about
   - ☐ a. Lincoln's attempt to fight
     off Booth's attack.
   - ☐ b. Booth's escape from
     the theater.
   - ☐ c. medical aid given to Lincoln.

8. When Booth shouted, "Sic Semper
   Tyrannis," he was
   - ☐ a. referring to himself.
   - ☐ b. calling Lincoln a tyrant.
   - ☐ c. making a reference to
     his enemies.

9. The author develops this
   article through
   - ☐ a. personal opinions.
   - ☐ b. vivid descriptions.
   - ☐ c. scientific facts.

10. We may conclude that Booth
    - ☐ a. planned his escape
      carefully in advance.
    - ☐ b. hated all presidents.
    - ☐ c. was not captured near
      the theater.

Canned or Frozen

Fruits that are to be canned or frozen must be picked at the right time. Carefully picked fruits have the right flavor for processing. Much of the processing today is done by factory machines. Very little of the fruit is touched by plant workers.

The work begins the same whether the fruits are to be canned or frozen. At the plant, the fruits are sorted into sizes by machine. Next, they are washed. Some fruits, such as apples, pears, and pineapples, are then peeled and cored by machine. Then they move along belts to plant workers. The workers do any other peeling or cutting. Machines remove the pits and seeds before the fruits are cut up. The fruit is cut in various ways, in halves, slices, or pieces. Plant workers then remove any bad pieces.

Next, cans or glass jars are filled with the fruit. Then they move along to machines that fill them up with the right amount of syrup or liquid. Next they go to machines that seal them. The sealed cans or jars are carefully cooked. Cooking time and temperature must be controlled to make sure that the fruits will keep without being refrigerated. The cans or jars are then cooled. They are stored in cool, dry warehouses until they are shipped to market.

Fruits to be frozen are usually packed with dry sugar. After they are prepared at the plant, they are packaged with more sugar or syrup and the packages are sealed. The packages are then quick frozen in special low-temperature chambers and stored at zero degrees or lower.

How you store processed fruits is important. Keep canned fruits in a place not more than 75 degrees. If you do this, the fruits will keep for a year or more. Once a can has been opened, the fruit should be placed in a refrigerator unless you are going to eat it right away.

Frozen fruits can be stored in an ice-cube section of a refrigerator. This will keep them for just a few days. If they are kept in a separate freezer section, most fruits will keep well for a few weeks. Frozen fruits taste best when they are stored in a freezer that is kept at zero degrees or lower. If you wish to use only a part of a package, be sure to put the rest of the package back in the freezer before it has thawed.

Recalling Facts

1. Carefully picked fruits
   have the right
   ☐ a. blossom.
   ☐ b. flavor.
   ☐ c. size.

2. Much of the processing
   today is done by factory
   ☐ a. bosses.
   ☐ b. machines.
   ☐ c. workers.

3. Fruits are sorted
   according to
   ☐ a. shape.
   ☐ b. size.
   ☐ c. taste.

4. After the fruit is
   sorted, it is
   ☐ a. dried.
   ☐ b. peeled.
   ☐ c. washed.

5. Canned fruits should
   be kept in a place that
   is not more than
   ☐ a. 75 degrees.
   ☐ b. 80 degrees.
   ☐ c. 85 degrees.

Understanding the Passage

6. It is not a good idea to
   can a fruit that is too
   ☐ a. colorful.
   ☐ b. ripe.
   ☐ c. small.

7. Before apples can be canned,
   they have to be
   ☐ a. bruised.
   ☐ b. peeled.
   ☐ c. polished.

8. This article hints that
   ☐ a. bad pieces of fruit
       are not canned.
   ☐ b. fruits are hard to
       can or freeze.
   ☐ c. plant workers carry
       many germs.

9. Cans or glass jars are heated
   to prevent the fruit from
   ☐ a. freezing.
   ☐ b. going bad.
   ☐ c. ripening.

10. If canned fruits are stored in a
    very warm place, they
    ☐ a. keep forever.
    ☐ b. spoil easily.
    ☐ c. start to grow.

Protein, carbohydrates, and fats are needed for a good diet. Along with water and fat, our bodies contain much protein. Protein is most important to a healthy body. Enzymes are made of protein. They help to keep the body working. Antibodies in the bloodstream are also made of protein. They fight off disease. The body also needs protein to build muscle. The muscles in turn hold the bone structure together. Muscles provide the strength to move and work. It's a good thing that most of us get enough protein.

But where is protein found? Meat, poultry, fish, milk, cheese, and eggs ● give us good amounts of it. Bread and cereal are also important sources. Vegetables, like soybeans, chick-peas, dry beans, and peanuts, are also good sources of protein. You do not have to load up on meat, poultry, or eggs to get enough protein in your diet. Eating cereal or vegetable foods with milk, cheese, or other animal protein can give you enough protein in your diet. For example, eat cereal with milk, rice with fish, or simply drink a glass of milk during a meal. Together, these foods provide the high quality protein the body needs.

Carbohydrates are the biggest source of energy. This group is made up ● of starches and sugars. Carbohydrates are mostly found in cereal grains, fruits, vegetables, potatoes, sweet potatoes, and vegetables like peas, dry beans, peanuts, and soybeans. Most other vegetables have smaller amounts of carbohydrates. In vegetables, the carbohydrates are usually in the form of starch. In fruits, they show up as sugar. Of course, candies, jams, and syrups are mostly sugar.

Fats give us energy. They add flavor and variety to foods. Fats carry vitamins A, D, E, and K. Fats are also an important part of the cells which ● make up the body's tissues. Our body fat protects our important organs by surrounding them with a cushion. Fats are found in butter, margarine, shortening, salad oils, and cream. Most cheeses, mayonnaise, salad dressing, nuts, and bacon also have a good deal of fat.

A good and balanced diet will use foods from all three of the above groups. In the end, eating right pays off in a healthier body. You'll not only look better, but you will also feel better. Pay attention to what fuels your body.

Recalling Facts

1. Protein, carbohydrates, and
   fats are needed for a good
   - ☐ a. diet.
   - ☐ b. job.
   - ☐ c. rest.

2. Antibodies are found in the
   - ☐ a. brain.
   - ☐ b. blood.
   - ☐ c. heart.

3. Antibodies fight off
   - ☐ a. calories.
   - ☐ b. disease.
   - ☐ c. fat.

4. Which of the following is a
   good source of protein?
   - ☐ a. butter
   - ☐ b. meat
   - ☐ c. sugar

5. What is the biggest source
   of energy in our diet?
   - ☐ a. carbohydrates
   - ☐ b. protein
   - ☐ c. vitamins

Understanding the Passage

6. If we did not have antibodies
   in our blood, we would
   probably become
   - ☐ a. overweight.
   - ☐ b. sick.
   - ☐ c. tired.

7. Our bones are held together by
   - ☐ a. fats.
   - ☐ b. muscles.
   - ☐ c. protein.

8. Body fat is used by our bodies to
   - ☐ a. build muscles.
   - ☐ b. carry antibodies.
   - ☐ c. protect our organs.

9. Soybeans are a source of both
   protein and
   - ☐ a. carbohydrates.
   - ☐ b. minerals.
   - ☐ c. vitamins.

10. What is this article about?
   - ☐ a. disease, infection,
          and germs
   - ☐ b. protein, carbohydrates,
          and fats
   - ☐ c. vitamins, minerals,
          and protein

Cats are clean animals and easy to housebreak. A shallow pan or box can be covered with an inch or so of sand, sawdust, or litter. Litter can be bought at pet stores, supermarkets, and hardware stores. The pan should always be in the same place.

To teach a cat, one must watch it carefully. When it begins to search for one place after another, it must be put into its pan. The litter must be changed often, and the pan must be washed with soap and water every few days.

A cat will scratch to wear off its old claws. It will need a scratching post to reduce damage to furniture. Every time the cat claws at the furniture, the scratching post should be pointed out to it until it learns to use it without help.

A cat enjoys a soft ball, a toy mouse, or some other kind of toy. Such objects should be too large for the cat to swallow.

Most cats enjoy playing. They are independent animals, however, and play only when they feel like it.

Most cats refuse to be disciplined although they may understand "no." They learn their names quickly, and many will come when called. If a cat is told what to do and it likes the trick, it will learn to do it.

A cat should be confined to the house, especially at night. Cats that are allowed to roam disturb the neighbors with their crying and fighting. A female cat should never be allowed to roam during her mating season.

Proper care usually will eliminate the threat of disease or injury. Unusual symptoms should be watched for, and visits to the veterinarian should be regular. A cat must be vaccinated early against rabies and other serious diseases.

A cat will lick its fur to clean it. As it licks, it will swallow hairs that form little feltlike balls in its stomach and intestines.

Although hair balls can be prevented by brushing a cat daily, some will form anyway. A veterinarian can prescribe a remedy to help a cat eliminate the hair.

A cat should never be dropped because it can be seriously injured. Cats do not always land on their feet as many people think. They also are not blessed with nine lives as is sometimes thought. Cats are extremely agile, but should never be tested on this point by humans.

Recalling Facts

1. A cat's litter box must be washed with soap and water
   - ☐ a. every few days.
   - ☐ b. once a week.
   - ☐ c. once a month.

2. A cat scratches objects to
   - ☐ a. sharpen its claws.
   - ☐ b. wear down its claws.
   - ☐ c. exercise.

3. Cats should not be given playthings that are too
   - ☐ a. small.
   - ☐ b. large.
   - ☐ c. rough.

4. The author says that cats are
   - ☐ a. proud.
   - ☐ b. quick.
   - ☐ c. independent.

5. Cats should be vaccinated to prevent
   - ☐ a. rabies.
   - ☐ b. heartworm.
   - ☐ c. cancer.

Understanding the Passage

6. A cat will learn a trick if it
   - ☐ a. is fed immediately before the trick.
   - ☐ b. is scolded when it fails to do the trick.
   - ☐ c. enjoys what it is doing.

7. To housebreak a cat, the owner should
   - ☐ a. change the litter in the box every few hours.
   - ☐ b. keep the litter box in the same place.
   - ☐ c. reward the cat if it uses the litter box.

8. Cats should be kept indoors at night because they
   - ☐ a. are noisy.
   - ☐ b. may catch cold.
   - ☐ c. may run away.

9. A veterinarian is
   - ☐ a. a pet store owner.
   - ☐ b. an animal trainer.
   - ☐ c. an animal doctor.

10. We can conclude that cats
    - ☐ a. are very difficult to housebreak.
    - ☐ b. are intelligent and easy to train.
    - ☐ c. require a minimum of care.

45　Brush It Away

Do you know how to really clean your teeth? Do you always do a good job? The goal is to remove all plaque. Plaque is always forming. It coats your teeth. You must do a good cleaning job at least once a day, preferably at night. It takes five to ten minutes to do a good job. To clean your teeth properly, you need a good brush.

Today some people use electric toothbrushes. They are pleasant to use and are most helpful to handicapped people. But, you can clean your teeth thoroughly with a regular toothbrush.

To make sure you are doing the job right, there are a few rules to follow. ● Replace toothbrushes often. A worn-out brush cleans poorly. Its bent bristles can hurt gums.

Use toothpaste or powder. These help clean the teeth. They are refreshing and leave a pleasant taste after brushing. Most toothpaste contains fluoride which helps stop tooth decay. The substance in toothpaste called abrasives helps clean teeth but may also wear away tooth enamel. Toothpastes vary in the amount of abrasives they contain. Check with your dentist about the brand you use. Baking soda or a mixture of baking soda and salt can clean ● teeth well and save you money, too.

The use of dental floss is good for removing food from places your toothbrush cannot reach. If you have not been using floss, it may seem hard at first. It gets easier with daily practice. It is a good idea to check with your dentist to be sure that you are flossing correctly. When using floss, be careful not to cut into the gums.

Plaque causes tooth decay. A good light and a mirror will show up plaque if you have any. Your drugstore sells wafers or liquids that you can use for this same purpose. These stain plaque red or blue so that you can ● see it. By staining the plaque after brushing and flossing, you can see which areas you may have missed. Brush these areas again.

There are other aids which can be used to help clean between teeth. Your drugstore sells special toothpicks which can be used to help scrape away plaque. Water sprays are available, too. These are used to help remove loose bits of food from between the teeth. Both of these should be used with care to avoid damaging the gums. None of these aids replaces the toothbrush for removing plaque.

Recalling Facts

1. You brush your teeth to remove
   - ☐ a. enamel.
   - ☐ b. plaque.
   - ☐ c. stains.

2. You should brush your teeth at least
   - ☐ a. once a day.
   - ☐ b. every other day.
   - ☐ c. once a week.

3. The best time to brush your teeth is
   - ☐ a. morning.
   - ☐ b. noon.
   - ☐ c. night.

4. Most toothpastes contain
   - ☐ a. calcium.
   - ☐ b. fluoride.
   - ☐ c. plaque.

5. Abrasives wear away the
   - ☐ a. gums.
   - ☐ b. old fillings.
   - ☐ c. tooth enamel.

Understanding the Passage

6. A worn-out toothbrush can cause
   - ☐ a. gum damage.
   - ☐ b. skin problems.
   - ☐ c. tooth decay.

7. Toothpaste usually
   - ☐ a. is expensive.
   - ☐ b. smells bad.
   - ☐ c. tastes good.

8. Baking soda is used in place of
   - ☐ a. dental floss.
   - ☐ b. mouthwash.
   - ☐ c. toothpaste.

9. Dental floss removes food from
   - ☐ a. between the teeth.
   - ☐ b. inside the lip.
   - ☐ c. under the tongue.

10. We can see that many tooth problems are caused by
   - ☐ a. diet.
   - ☐ b. fluoride.
   - ☐ c. plaque.

46   A Toast to the Toaster

Electric toasters have come a long way since the 1920s. Today, you can even choose the color of your toast. Modern toasters come in two styles. They are either upright or horizontal types. The upright toasters hold the bread in an up-and-down position. In the horizontal type, the slices lie flat.

There are two kinds of upright toasters. The first type holds two or four slices of bread. Other upright models have ovens. These ovens can toast, warm, or bake.

The first kind of upright toaster has often been called an automatic pop-up toaster. Some people even call them wall toasters. They toast bread, frozen waffles, and thin pastries without toppings or fillings. They are simple machines and are easy to work. The bread carriage has an outside control knob. When the knob is worked, the carriage moves up and down inside the toast wells. The carriage works an on-off switch. The heating elements in an upright toaster are made of fine wires. These are placed on both sides of each toast well. When electricity flows through the wires, they give off heat for toasting. A thermostat inside the toaster is hooked up to an outside toast-color control. The control lets you choose the toasting time.

The second upright model is both a toaster and a small oven. These models have toast wells, bread carriages, and toast-color controls. Plus, they have special doors and controls for baking and warming.

Horizontal toasters are either reflector models or toaster ovens. Reflector models toast and warm. Toaster ovens toast, warm, and bake. Both have built-in two and four slice sizes and have a front door or opening. Both can handle most bread sizes.

Choose your toaster carefully. Look for a seal of approval from an independent testing laboratory. This seal is important. It lets you know that this toaster is as safe as possible. The seal might be on the toaster. It may also be on the packing carton. Such a seal shows, among other things, that the toaster has a two-pole switch. This switch is a safety point. It stops a child from getting a shock. Even if a child puts his hand inside the toasting chamber while the toaster is plugged in, he should not get a shock.

The next time you're in the market for a toaster, look for the seal of safety.

Recalling Facts

1. Electric toasters have come a
   long way since the
   □ a. 1860s.
   □ b. 1880s.
   □ c. 1920s.

2. Some toasters can warm and
   □ a. bake.
   □ b. broil.
   □ c. fry.

3. The heating elements in a
   toaster are made of fine
   □ a. screws.
   □ b. threads.
   □ c. wires.

4. Horizontal toasters are either
   reflector models or
   □ a. control toasters.
   □ b. pop-up broilers.
   □ c. toaster ovens.

5. A two-pole switch on a toaster
   stops a child from getting a
   □ a. burn.
   □ b. cut.
   □ c. shock.

Understanding the Passage

6. Toasters
   □ a. come in different styles.
   □ b. have not changed since 1900.
   □ c. serve one person at a time.

7. The pop-up toaster is
   also called a
   □ a. camp toaster.
   □ b. serving toaster.
   □ c. wall toaster.

8. In order to toast a piece of
   bread, you need
   □ a. heat.
   □ b. sugar.
   □ c. water.

9. A thermostat controls the
   □ a. color of the toast.
   □ b. size of the toast.
   □ c. weight of the toast.

10. How many types of horizontal
    toasters are there?
    □ a. one
    □ b. two
    □ c. three

47

Safety First

There are many things around the house that can hurt a child. For example, baby's crib and playpen are not always safe. Parents who think every crib or playpen is danger free should think again. Sad but true, some furniture companies forget about safety.

When choosing a crib or a playpen, be sure that the slats are spaced no more than two-and-one-half inches apart. With slats like these, the baby cannot catch his head between them. Be careful, too, of loose slats that could come out. A missing slat leaves a gap. The infant's head could easily get caught.

Even thin plastic, the kind you get from the cleaners, can be a very dangerous thing in a baby's world. It should never be used to cover a crib mattress. It should not be left where a baby could grab it and pull it over his face. A baby has no defense against this kind of thin, sticky plastic. The plastic can cling to his mouth and nose, cutting off his air supply.

We know that every home contains a great number of things that are tempting to a baby. These objects can do a lot of harm when baby is in the hand-to-mouth stage. Before putting a child down on the floor to play, check the floor carefully. Keep things like buttons, beads, pins, screws, or anything small out of baby's reach. Look out for anything small enough to fit in the infant's mouth. Small objects can get lodged in the throat and cut off the child's air supply.

Toys are not always safe either. The most dangerous toys for a child under three are those small enough to swallow. Do not let a young child play with marbles or small plastic toys. Avoid toys that come apart easily. Do not buy stuffed animals or dolls with tiny button eyes or ornaments that can be easily pulled off. Never let a child chew on balloons. He might bite off a piece and choke.

Do not feed a young child popcorn, nuts, or small, hard candies. Doctors find that young children do not know how to eat things like these. These foods can easily get sucked into the windpipe instead of going to the stomach. The same is true of pills. Use liquid medicine. If pills must be used, they should be crushed.

Recalling Facts

1. The slats of a crib or playpen should be spaced no more than
   - ☐ a. 2½ inches apart.
   - ☐ b. 5 inches apart.
   - ☐ c. 5½ inches apart.

2. Which of the following should never be used to cover a crib mattress?
   - ☐ a. linen sheets
   - ☐ b. thin plastic
   - ☐ c. woolen blankets

3. You should not buy stuffed animals that have
   - ☐ a. colored ribbons.
   - ☐ b. large feet.
   - ☐ c. tiny button eyes.

4. Which of the following toys might prove dangerous to a small child?
   - ☐ a. balloons
   - ☐ b. rattles
   - ☐ c. puppets

5. A young child should not be allowed to eat
   - ☐ a. bread.
   - ☐ b. spaghetti.
   - ☐ c. nuts.

Understanding the Passage

6. What is the main thought of this article?
   - ☐ a. Children learn how to walk before they run.
   - ☐ b. Doctors know that children do not know how to eat popcorn.
   - ☐ c. Some things around the house are harmful to children.

7. We can see that young children like to
   - ☐ a. cry a lot before they go to bed.
   - ☐ b. put things in their mouths.
   - ☐ c. stay in one place.

8. Thin plastic can cause a baby to
   - ☐ a. sleep.
   - ☐ b. smile.
   - ☐ c. smother.

9. Hard candies can make a child
   - ☐ a. breathe.
   - ☐ b. choke.
   - ☐ c. whine.

10. For a child, swallowing liquid medicine is easier than swallowing
    - ☐ a. pills.
    - ☐ b. syrup.
    - ☐ c. water.

48

Take Your Pick!

Of all the foods we know, fruit is one of the most healthful. It is also one of the most tasty foods. Almost everyone enjoys fruit. Fruit is grown in almost every part of the world. There are hundreds of different kinds of fruits. And there are thousands of different varieties. In the United States alone, there are several hundred types of apples.

In general though, there are three separate groups. There are tropical fruits. These are most important. In this group, we have bananas and pine-apples. They are shipped from tropical countries and are eaten all over the world.

Next come the subtropical fruits. The most important of these are the citrus fruits. Oranges, tangerines, limes, and grapefruit are favorites. Other fruits in this class are figs, dates, and olives.

The last group comes from the temperate zone. In this group are pears, apples, grapes, and plums. Many kinds of berries fit this group, too.

Fruits are very important to the human diet. Besides being tasty, they provide important acids, salts, and vitamins. Also, they are easy to digest. Nutrition experts say that the more fruit people eat, the healthier they become.

Down through the centuries fruit has played a part in tales and history. In a Greek myth, Hercules sent Atlas to pick "golden apples" to pay for a crime. Today we believe these golden apples were oranges. During the 1700s, British ships began to carry limes. It was found that sailors who drank the lime juice did not get sick. Since that time, British sailors have been called "limeys."

The peach also has an exciting history. It has been a world traveler. Its journey began many, many centuries ago. Peaches were first grown in China. From China, traders of long ago carried peach trees to Persia. From there, Alexander the Great brought the fruit to Europe. From Europe, Spanish ships carried peaches to the New World.

Through the years, fruit trees and plants have been improved. Today's fruits are bigger. They also taste better. Different kinds of fruits are often being bred. We now have fruit that can travel to all parts of the world and still stay fresh. Even after traveling for some time, these new fruits keep the vitamins and minerals that are so good for our diet. Fruit will always be prized as a basic food that now can be enjoyed the whole year round.

Recalling Facts

1. Of all the foods we know, fruit is one of the most
   - ☐ a. colorful.
   - ☐ b. healthful.
   - ☐ c. plentiful.

2. How many separate groups of fruits are there?
   - ☐ a. two
   - ☐ b. three
   - ☐ c. four

3. Which of the following is a tropical fruit?
   - ☐ a. an apple
   - ☐ b. a banana
   - ☐ c. a pear

4. Fruits are easy to
   - ☐ a. digest.
   - ☐ b. plant.
   - ☐ c. serve.

5. During the 1700s, British ships began to carry
   - ☐ a. dates.
   - ☐ b. limes.
   - ☐ c. plums.

Understanding the Passage

6. What type of climate are pineapples grown in?
   - ☐ a. cold and dry
   - ☐ b. hot and humid
   - ☐ c. snowy and wet

7. Citrus fruits come from the
   - ☐ a. subtropics.
   - ☐ b. temperate zone.
   - ☐ c. tropics.

8. Most people think fruits
   - ☐ a. grow slowly.
   - ☐ b. bruise easily.
   - ☐ c. taste good.

9. British sailors have been called "limeys" because, at one time, they
   - ☐ a. drank lime juice.
   - ☐ b. lived only on limes.
   - ☐ c. refused to ship limes.

10. Today's fruits
   - ☐ a. like a lot of rain.
   - ☐ b. stay fresh a long time.
   - ☐ c. need a lot of fertilizer.

49 Buying a Canary

Canaries are a type of small, yellow finch. They are known for their singing, and they make entertaining pets.

When you buy your canary, select one that is healthy. If you want a singing bird, make sure it is a male and can sing before you buy it. Properly trained singing canaries cost more than untrained ones.

Most young canaries learn to sing by listening to older birds. If your bird cannot sing, you will need a singing bird or a canary tape or record to teach it.

Your canary will need a cage with perches, a bird bath, and containers for food and water. You can buy cages, equipment, and food in pet or variety stores.

A cage about fourteen inches square and eighteen inches high will house one or two birds. A larger cage will give your canary more room for play and exercise.

Hang the cage at about eye-level height away from drafts. Cover the cage with a cloth at night. Birds like privacy when they sleep.

Clean the perches and the cage's floor at least once a week or more often if necessary. If you cover the floor with paper, you can replace the paper when it becomes soiled.

Keep food and fresh drinking water available at all times. Check the food daily to make sure that the container has seed in it, not just empty husks. Change the drinking water every day. Clean the food and water containers at least twice a week.

Birds have no teeth so they eat gravel to grind their food into small pieces. Keep gravel in the cage at all times in a separate container from the food or on the cage floor.

Your canary should have water for bathing once a day in summer and two or three times a week in winter. Empty and clean the bird bath after each use.

Your canary should be easy to tame. Talk softly to it when you are near its cage. It will soon get used to you and feel safe in its new home.

Birds molt once a year, usually in late July and August. When your canary is molting, it may be less active than usual. Do not disturb it any more than necessary during this time.

Canaries will mate in captivity. If you wish to raise young birds, you should see a pet shop for information.

Recalling Facts

1. Canaries are a type of
   - ☐ a. finch.
   - ☐ b. sparrow.
   - ☐ c. wren.

2. The author mentions using a cage that is 14 inches square by
   - ☐ a. 12 inches high.
   - ☐ b. 16 inches high.
   - ☐ c. 18 inches high.

3. Canary cages should be cleaned every
   - ☐ a. day.
   - ☐ b. week.
   - ☐ c. month.

4. To digest their food, canaries eat
   - ☐ a. seed husks.
   - ☐ b. gravel.
   - ☐ c. wood chips.

5. Canaries usually molt during
   - ☐ a. April.
   - ☐ b. July.
   - ☐ c. November.

Understanding the Passage

6. During the time that a canary is molting, it should be
   - ☐ a. put in a warm place.
   - ☐ b. given extra food.
   - ☐ c. left alone.

7. The author implies that
   - ☐ a. birds will not breed in small cages.
   - ☐ b. only male canaries can sing.
   - ☐ c. female canaries are more active than male birds.

8. Cages should be covered at night so that the birds will
   - ☐ a. have some privacy.
   - ☐ b. not be chilled.
   - ☐ c. not sleep during the daytime.

9. The reader can infer that
   - ☐ a. canaries can be taught to sing in the home.
   - ☐ b. young canaries learn to fly at three months of age.
   - ☐ c. canaries do not normally mate in captivity.

10. The author stresses the need for
    - ☐ a. buying the correct food for a canary.
    - ☐ b. keeping the canary's cage, water, and food clean.
    - ☐ c. letting the canary leave the cage for exercise.

Most homeowners know that termites can hurt the wood in their homes. Over the years, these insects have caused great damage over much of the United States. If termites are found in the home, there is no cause for panic. They can be controlled.

Underground termites live in large groups called colonies. The workers and soldiers spend their entire lives underground or completely buried in wood. Thus, they are rarely seen. Termites need high humidity in order to live. They keep their nests humid by using moisture from the soil. But, sometimes there is enough moisture in the wood by itself. Because underground termites do not like dry air, they remain buried. So, the damage they cause goes unnoticed.

Winged termites inside a house are almost a sure sign of trouble. They are easy to spot. They have yellow-brown or black bodies. Their two pairs of wings are of equal size. Winged ants have two pairs of unequal sized wings. Also, termites have thick waistlines; ants have hourglass figures.

Once they nest, the termites shed their wings. Wings are often found beneath doors or windows. Because the winged termites are drawn to light, their wings may be found around light fixtures. If you find wings inside the house, you can guess that termites have moved in.

Damage to wood cannot be seen unless the outside of the wood is stripped away. When it is, many paths are found in the wood. Workers may usually be seen when a piece of damaged wood is studied. Both the workers and soldiers are wingless and grayish white in color. The workers feed on the wood while the soldiers guard the colony. The two forms look alike, but the soldiers have larger heads and jaws.

The only sure way to stop termite attacks or to get rid of them is to cut off their source of moisture. Without moisture, a colony will die. Keep in mind that termites can attack dry wood. They can do this by bringing in their own moisture from the soil.

In some places termites are common. Homeowners can make sure they are safe from attack by calling a pest control company. This kind of company first checks the house. It then does whatever is needed to kill the termites. The cost of this treatment depends on the amount of work to be done. But it is better to be safe than sorry.

Recalling Facts

1. Underground termites live in large groups called
   - ☐ a. colonies.
   - ☐ b. cities.
   - ☐ c. gangs.

2. Sometimes worker and soldier termites spend their whole lives buried in
   - ☐ a. clay.
   - ☐ b. rock.
   - ☐ c. wood.

3. Termites get the moisture they need from
   - ☐ a. nearby ponds.
   - ☐ b. the soil.
   - ☐ c. wells.

4. Winged termites are either yellow-brown or
   - ☐ a. black.
   - ☐ b. orange.
   - ☐ c. white.

5. What color are the worker and soldier termites?
   - ☐ a. brownish black
   - ☐ b. grayish white
   - ☐ c. yellow-black

Understanding the Passage

6. Termites are a type of
   - ☐ a. fungus.
   - ☐ b. insect.
   - ☐ c. mineral.

7. In order to live, termites need
   - ☐ a. sunlight.
   - ☐ b. sugar.
   - ☐ c. water.

8. Some termites are hard to spot because they
   - ☐ a. only come out at night.
   - ☐ b. live underground.
   - ☐ c. travel very fast.

9. We can see from this article that some termites can
   - ☐ a. fly.
   - ☐ b. hop.
   - ☐ c. jump.

10. Termites and ants
    - ☐ a. have different body shapes.
    - ☐ b. live side by side.
    - ☐ c. often attack and kill each other.

Progress Graph (26–50)

Directions: Write your comprehension score in the box under the selection number. Then put an x on the line above each box to show your reading time and words-per-minute reading rate.

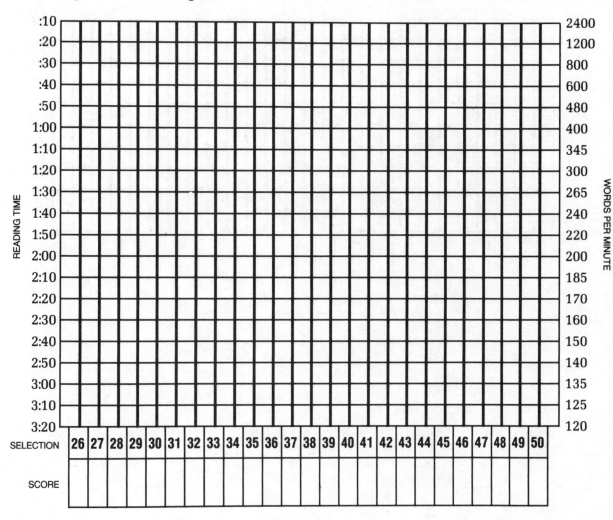

READING TIME		WORDS PER MINUTE
:10		2400
:20		1200
:30		800
:40		600
:50		480
1:00		400
1:10		345
1:20		300
1:30		265
1:40		240
1:50		220
2:00		200
2:10		185
2:20		170
2:30		160
2:40		150
2:50		140
3:00		135
3:10		125
3:20		120

SELECTION: 26 27 28 29 30 31 32 33 34 35 36 37 38 39 40 41 42 43 44 45 46 47 48 49 50

SCORE

Pacing Graph

Directions: In the boxes labeled "Pace" along the bottom of the graph, write your words-per-minute rate. On the vertical line above each box, put an x to indicate your comprehension score.

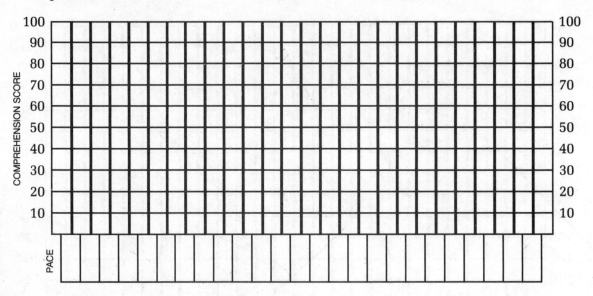